LOOKING DEEP

Terry Bradshaw

LOOKING DEEP

with Buddy Martin

CB

CONTEMPORARY
BOOKS

CHICAGO · NEW YORK

Library of Congress Cataloging-in-Publication Data

Bradshaw, Terry.
    Looking deep / Terry Bradshaw with Buddy Martin.
       p.   cm.
    ISBN 0-8092-4266-4 : $17.95
      1. Football players—United States—Biography.
2. Pittsburgh Steelers (Football team)   I. Bradshaw, Terry.
II. Martin, Buddy.   III. Title.
GV939.B68A3   1989
796.332'092—dc20
[B]   89-15818
                                           CIP

Published by Contemporary Books, Inc.
180 North Michigan Avenue, Chicago, Illinois 60601
Manufactured in the United States of America
International Standard Book Number: 0-8092-4266-4

Published simultaneously in Canada by Beaverbooks, Ltd.
195 Allstate Parkway, Valleywood Business Park
Markham, Ontario L3R 4T8 Canada

To my mom and dad, Novis and Bill Bradshaw

CONTENTS

PREFACE

Writing a book wasn't high on my list of priorities when Buddy Martin called me in February 1986. First off, I'm not a kiss-and-tell kind of guy. Secondly, I already had enough happening in my life, what with my job at CBS-TV, my bride of one month, Charla, and an upcoming relocation from my Louisiana ranch to Texas.

In fact, about the last thing I wanted to do was to write a book. It's not my style to criticize my teammates, knock my parents, or make revealing statements about close friends that would be embarrassing to them. In today's book market, that seems to be what publishers are demanding. Having already gone through an ordeal with some of my former teammates who took exception to my commentaries when I worked for KDKA-TV in Pittsburgh, I didn't want to stir up those emotions again.

It was only after talking with my coauthor, who convinced me that the best way to deal with my anger and frustration in my past was to confront it, that I agreed to write my autobiography. I wasn't even aware that I harbored any bitterness about my past, but evidently Buddy was able to spot that in me. Buddy was right. So I am very grateful to him.

From the outset there were strict guidelines, because I wanted to write a tasteful book that kids could read. I didn't want to go to church and hear my pastor offering prayers for me before the congregation because of what he had read in the book. While at times it was a painful process, I have to admit it has been therapeutic. When my anger surfaced during the interviewing process, sometimes I would rant and rave and shout obscenities into the tape recorder. Later that night I would change the language, then wake up in the morning and change it again. Although those fits of frustration are not evident in the final manuscript, I did benefit from the purging of my anger.

It wasn't a pleasant experience, either, hopping a plane from Dallas to New York so that I might parade before a half-dozen editors and try to convince them that my story was worth telling. I could see in their eyes that they felt this book was PG-rated, that it wasn't going to be as controversial as the works of Jim McMahon and Brian Bosworth. When they found out that I didn't have any scandalous stories about sex or drugs or rock & roll, they lost interest.

What I learned in doing this book is that it's tough to deal with your true feelings when you know they are being laid out in print for all the world to see, and when you are conforming to rigid guidelines of taste—and all the while trying to be as honest as possible. It was a tough balancing act and required great tolerance between coauthors, especially when some publishers kept insisting that only controversy would sell books.

At the same time, I didn't want to sugarcoat everything. Everybody has certain negative points, and I'm no exception. So rather than distort the picture by omitting certain facts, I tried to deal honestly with every facet of my own life, including my struggles to overcome the curse of a "dumb" image and my conflicts with Chuck Noll.

Everything came together when Shari Lesser Wenk of Contemporary Books entered the picture. She understood the concept from the beginning and was willing to offer us the kind of control over the content that others were not. She, too, believed that a story could be told interestingly without being told totally at the expense of others. This book might not have ever been completed without the good faith of Shari and Nancy Crossman of Contemporary Books, who shared our vision.

—Terry Bradshaw

INTRODUCTION

I started out to write a book about Terry Bradshaw and gained a lifetime friend. After knowing him personally for only two hours, I saw a side of this man that fascinated me—a side which had not been revealed by the media during his fourteen-plus seasons as a quarterback for the Pittsburgh Steelers.

The first things that attracted my attention were his sense of humor, his candor, and his disavowment of his own celebrity. Most of his humor was directed at himself, and he laughed harder than anybody else at his own flaws. Perhaps that's the reason why people have underestimated his intelligence. Believe me, after three years of working on *Looking Deep*, I can attest to the fact that Terry Bradshaw not only isn't "dumb" but is one of the brightest athletes I've encountered in thirty years of writing about the men who play boys' games.

For the past three years I've seen Bradshaw at his worst and at his best. At his best he can be downright charming, effervescent, and magnetic. Truthfully, there wasn't much bad to see, except maybe an occasional hook of his drive into the rough. Whether on the set of "The NFL Today" at CBS, babysitting with Rachel, his newborn baby daughter, or teeing up at Los Colinas in Irving, Texas, Terry never shut me out of any part of his life during the writing of this book. For that, I am eternally grateful. At his insistence, once we began the interviewing process we spent as much time together as possible. "Come to Dallas," he insisted, "and get to know me." Usually they were four- or five-day sessions— sometimes shorter, sometimes longer.

We began at his ranch in Grand Cane, Louisiana; then we shifted to his apartment in Irving; to his rental house in Irving; and, finally, to his new home in Roanoke, Texas. In between, we worked on the manuscript in San Francisco; New Orleans; Chicago; Pasadena, California; San Diego; Houston; New York; Denver; Steamboat Springs, Colorado; and Colorado Springs, Colorado.

We played golf, cards, and pool—a lot of golf. We fished, listened to country music (he introduced me to the songs of Randy Travis, Ricky Van Shelton, and K. T. Oslin), sang, laughed a lot, talked about God, wondered aloud about life and death, played with baby daughter Rachel on the floor, danced, ate fried catfish (the best I ever tasted), and smoked cigars.

At the very moment Terry received Pete Elliott's phone call telling him he had been elected to the Pro Football Hall of Fame, we were throwing the football in his backyard—my fingers were numb from catching his bullet passes. I had never seen him so overwhelmed with joy. But it was not always fun. On occasion, when delving deep into the painful subjects of broken marriages, or failed friendships, or rejection by his coach, Chuck Noll, he became depressed. But the depression usually lasted only for a few hours, or the remainder of the night, and he was back to his bubbly self the next morning.

Through the hospitality of Charla Bradshaw, I was a frequent overnight guest at both the Bradshaw home in Irving and the house in Roanoke for several days at a time. While having a houseguest is always burdensome, Charla was always gracious to me, allowing me to observe candid closeups of this complex yet simple man in the comfortable and natural environs of home.

During that period in 1986 and 1987, I saw him as an expectant father, new parent, ex-athlete, husband, businessman, golfer, friend, comic, country singer, couch potato, chef, PR man, and pool shark. He shared the deepest, most intimate secrets of his life in our interviews. That good faith exemplifies the mutual trust and friendship we developed and which I shall always treasure.

As you will see in these pages, Terry Bradshaw is a funloving, caring, multidimensional man. At Terry's 40th birthday party in Roanoke, his brother, Gary, asked me: "How did you know which Terry you were interviewing?" I saw only one personality with numerous facets: the man-child who delights in taunting his friends with pranks; the fierce competitor who instinctively reacts to the quest before him; the insecure athlete who broods over his inadequacies as a businessman and provider (unjustifiably, I might add); and the man with the teddy-bear heart who isn't afraid to show his love, whether embracing his baby girl, kissing his wife, or throwing his arm around a male friend to say good-bye.

As his traveling companion on a half-dozen trips, I observed how people reacted to Terry Bradshaw all over America and learned about the demands placed on a high-profile personality. It seemed to me Bradshaw was more popular than when he was a player. But fame is a two-edged sword. I saw him accosted by fans in airports, restaurants, ball parks, parking lots, hotel lobbies, and on golf courses. Usually the people were asking for autographs, although on occasion they wanted to express their annoyance with Bradshaw for defeating their favorite team. Once, when we drove his pickup truck to a garbage dump in Dallas to unload some refuse, the attendant didn't want to let Terry in because he had beaten the guy's beloved Cowboys in two Super Bowls.

Only once did I see Terry flatly refuse to sign an autograph. We had traveled all night from New York to Dallas after a whirlwind tour of book publishers in New York, a trip during which Terry's briefcase was pilfered by a yet-unapprehended thief. After just two hours' sleep, we were about to board a plane at Love Field in Dallas for a flight to Houston early the next morning. As we walked briskly through the terminal, a middle-aged businessman took dead aim on Terry. Not only did he want an autograph, but he was going to offer a little of his sarcastic humor at this ungodly hour when we both were overcome with fatigue and in no mood for jokes. "Well," the intruder said in his Texas drawl, extending his hand with pen and paper, "if it isn't Roger Staubach!"

Roger Staubach is a friend of Bradshaw's and one of the quarterbacks he most admires. But when you live in Dallas and are so often a target of mock derision by Cowboy fans, there is a limit to your capacity for humor—especially at 7 A.M.

"Do you know what I did to the last jerk who said that to me?" Bradshaw scolded, and the man turned and hightailed it. Terry's friendly puppy-dog public demeanor often invites intrusion by total strangers. Bradshaw is a guy you think you know when you see him for the first time, sort of like a next-door neighbor you haven't spoken to in a while.

"Put that in the book," Bradshaw said of the Dallas incident. "I want people to see what it's like." But I would be remiss if I didn't also mention the relaxed and warm exchanges Terry had with others: an oyster shucker in New Orleans; a black man at a stoplight in Harlem who, upon spotting a familiar face in the car next to him, simply raised his clenched right fist in salute to the former Steeler quarterback; Gene, the limousine driver in New York City, who felt bad because Terry's briefcase had been ripped off and feared that the thief may have stolen it from the car he was supposed to be guarding.

Our lives have changed somewhat over these three years. Terry became a father for the first time and was anxiously awaiting baby number two as this book was going to press. I lost my father, Marty Martin. Terry lost a beloved grandmother. The Bradshaws built a beautiful new home, hard by a man-made lake stocked with bass and catfish. As we put the finishing touches on *Looking Deep*, Terry's life appeared full and he was happier than I'd ever seen him. But there was a certain sense of melancholy for both of us, much the way a person feels when coming to the end of a long and exhilarating journey. I am richer for having made such extraordinary new friends as Charla and Terry. Hopefully, these pages will bring to life the Terry Bradshaw that I have come to know so intimately and hold in such high esteem.

—Buddy Martin

ACKNOWLEDGMENTS

We want to thank our wives, Charla Bradshaw and Joan Martin, who balance our checkbooks, not to mention our lives, as well as a few other friends who were instrumental in bringing various aspects of this project to fruition.

When you review the life of a person, there are many minute details that are difficult to remember. So when memories were foggy or none of the details were available in print, we sought the help of the following people to reconstruct events: former *Pittsburgh Post-Gazette* sports columnist Phil Musick, who covered almost every game during the 14-year span and was especially helpful in tracking down former Steelers; Glenn Sheeley of the *Atlanta Journal-Constitution*, who covered the Steelers toward the end of the Bradshaw era for the *Pittsburgh Press* and was of great assistance in proofreading; Ed Boucette, currently the Steelers beat writer for the *Post-Gazette*, whose advice on the manuscript and help in updating material was invaluable; former *Post-Gazette* sports editor John Clendenon, who so graciously granted the use of the newspaper's library; *Press* sports editor Russ Brown, who also shared his clip files;

Florida Times-Union sportswriter Niko Van Thyn, a classmate of Bradshaw's at Woodlawn High in Shreveport and at Louisiana Tech, who was able to track the early years and make some critical refinements; American Football Conference Director of Information Pete Abitante, who shipped us play-by-play sheets of the Super Bowls and numerous national newspaper articles; the Pittsburgh Steelers publicity department, for statistical details; and Nancy Karpan, who assisted in transcribing the tapes.

Morale ebbs and flows when you spend three years working on a book, and most helpful in boosting our spirits were Joe Williams, Tommy and Rhonda Vickers, Ron Zappolo, and Walt Tomooka of Denver; Dick Compton and Norm Bulaich of Dallas–Fort Worth; Shirley and Armand Lovell of Ocala, Florida; *Chicago Tribune* sports editor Tom Patterson; Nancy and Verne Lundquist of Steamboat Springs, Colorado, and Dallas; Gil Shanley of Shreveport, Louisiana; Gene and Lorna Kissinger; and J. Haas of Conoco, who stood behind us from the beginning.

We owe a debt of gratitude to the numerous photographers from the Associated Press Bureau in Pittsburgh for the many fine action and candid photos they provided, as well as to *Denver Post* photographer John Leyba, who snapped the Martin-Bradshaw photo for the jacket.

Most of all, however, we would like to thank Shari Lesser Wenk, formerly an editor at Contemporary Books. She not only provided the perfect marriage between authors and publisher but also vigorously pursued the manuscript from its inception because she believed in it. Shari confesses to being "the biggest Terry Bradshaw fan you will ever meet"; we have since become Shari Lesser Wenk fans. Our thanks also go to Nancy Crossman of Contemporary Books, who worked diligently on crafting the finished product.

1

A BOUNCING FOOTBALL, THE IMMACULATE RECEPTION

Three Rivers Stadium just two days before Christmas 1972 was not a very likely setting for the birth of a juggernaut. But whenever I'm asked to pinpoint a pivotal event in the fortunes of the Pittsburgh Steelers, I usually bring up the last-second pass I threw against the Oakland Raiders that miraculously rebounded into the hands of Franco Harris and became one of the most controversial touchdowns in National Football League history. It's impossible not to believe in the power of destiny when you review the play known as The Immaculate Reception. Franco's truly remarkable catch must have been sent from heaven; there's no other way to explain how such an incredible thing happened except to say it was divine intervention.

Skill had very little to do with the success of that desperation pass. Yet that single bounce of a football and the resulting touchdown changed the face of pro football. Just three years earlier, the Steelers had won one game and lost thirteen. The Immaculate Reception vaulted the Steelers into their first American Football Conference title game and unleashed a dynasty: eight straight playoff appearances and

back-to-back Super Bowl victories twice—four championships in a six-year period.

The glory days for the Steelers were still two years ahead,
but we buried our past that day. Like a Texas League single
that starts a rally in baseball, The Immaculate Reception
was the one event that seemed to finally break a forty-year
tradition of football futility in Pittsburgh.

My role in the events of that dark, dreary day in Pittsburgh was more a testimony to coincidence than career
planning: here I was, about to release this pass which would
take a funny bounce and provide the Steelers with the impe-
tus for their biggest victory in franchise history. I was just
trying to survive. As I released the ball, I was feeling very
uncertain about the next few seconds of the Steelers' fate,
not to mention my own future as a young quarterback in his
third NFL season.

Of the thousands of ways the ball would eventually tum-
ble in my fourteen years as quarterback of the Pittsburgh
Steelers, this was going to be the weirdest. I had seen it
bounce almost every conceivable way as a kid as I threw it at
trees, off my bedroom ceiling, on the roof, off my brother's
swing set. But I had never seen a bounce like this one and
never would again in my playing career.

Pittsburgh. Pray tell, how did I get there in the first place?
Pittsburgh. So foreign to me as a college student at Louisiana Tech in 1970 that upon being drafted by the Steelers, I
had to race to the encyclopedia and look up its location. I
opened the book to a picture of this northeastern industrial
city and tried, in vain, to imagine myself, a country boy
from Louisiana, among all those smokestacks. Pittsburgh. A
city with a forty-year history of losing pro football teams. A
hard-nosed, blue-collar, shot-and-a-beer town without
much of an appetite for raw rookie quarterbacks. A city and
a team that had once discarded the great Johnny Unitas.
Pittsburgh. Home of the Steelers, a team with the ugliest
uniforms I had seen since I wore the red and black colors of
Oak Terrace Junior High in Shreveport.

Pittsburgh. Cold and dark and frightening to a boy from

the sunny South who had dreamed since the age of seven of playing quarterback in the NFL. Why must I be in Pittsburgh? Why not Dallas, or Houston, or Miami, or Atlanta, or New Orleans—places where you could see the sun this time of the year? On this December day the sun had already gone south for the winter. Playoff games in Pittsburgh were a novelty back then, but depressing December days like this were fairly routine.

Pittsburgh. Not a destination by design or a situation I could have envisioned for myself, even with the vivid imagination of a seven-year-old. Had it been left to my choice, Pittsburgh would have been The Road Not Taken, because this is not how I'd planned it. Nor was I prepared for this crisis: trying to beat the Oakland Raiders in the final seventy-two seconds of this postseason game when all odds seemed against it.

I was throwing the football like a bullet that late summer day in 1961 at Oak Terrace Junior High, street clothes and all. In my thirteen-year-old heart I was every bit as good as Bart Starr and Johnny Unitas, two of my heroes. I was always throwing. When I was about ten, I used to lie in bed at night, street light shining in my window, bouncing the football off my bedroom ceiling after my family was already in bed. After a while my dad would say, "Terry Paxton!" (My parents used my middle name when they scolded me.) "Stop bouncing that football! You're keeping everybody awake." I'd say, "Okay, Dad!" And as soon as I heard Dad snoring, I'd start bouncing the ball again. Thump. Thump. Thump. There were brown spots on my bedroom ceiling from my nighttime games of solitary pitch and catch, the residue of the cordovan shoe polish I used to waterproof my football. Dad had warned me that the ball had to last the entire year, so I did whatever I could to preserve the leather. Sometimes the ball didn't hold up under the beating; the laces would break. Then I'd take a shoestring from my sneakers and thread it through the ball with a coat hanger. The football was my favorite toy.

If I wasn't throwing the football, I was throwing anything I could grip. I was fascinated by the flight of objects and would experiment with rocks or even cow chips. I was first drawn more to a baseball, probably because it fit my hand. There weren't any of those undersized footballs around in those days, like the ones used today by the pee-wee leagues, and so my early success was with a baseball.

My interest in baseball was first whetted as a batboy for my father's industrial-league softball team. But I always preferred playing over watching, so I joined a Little League team when I was about eight. In my first baseball game they put me in right field because nobody hit the ball there. I was a terrible player; I couldn't catch a thing. Then one day in Camanche, Iowa, where we had moved from Shreveport, a postman saw me throwing the baseball on an old diamond near our house. He went and got a catcher's mitt and asked me to pitch to him. Turns out he coached a Little League team and asked me to pitch for him that summer. My older brother, Gary, was the team's catcher. I pitched a perfect game, a couple of no-hitters, and about a half-dozen shutouts. We wound up beating a team of older kids in a higher classification and I got carried off the field. Pretty heady stuff for a nine-year-old. But my first love was still football, a game in which I still had enjoyed absolutely no success.

The next Christmas, while we were still living in Iowa, Dad gave me a Sears, Roebuck football, full size, and I began teaching myself to throw it. I'd stand in front of the mirror checking out my form and posture, pretending I was an NFL quarterback. Then I'd go outside and see if I could make it spiral, a task that was quite difficult because the footballs were so fat back then. It wasn't until the sixth grade, when we finally moved back to Shreveport, in 1959, that my passing began to develop. I wasn't on a team then, but in P.E. class we had those skinny rubber footballs that you could really gun. I found the best way to throw it was to put my index finger on the point and spread the rest of my fingers around it. It was through learning to throw those pointy footballs in P.E. that I would develop my style for passing the

J5V as well as throwing the javelin in high school and, eventually, for throwing the NFL ball.

The coach had picked only one kid out of the seventh grade to play on the junior high team, and it wasn't me. So I joined a Pop Warner League that year with the rest of the rejects. At least they let me play quarterback. The next year, 1961, we moved again; I changed junior high schools and tried out for the Oak Terrace team as an eighth grader. But my luck didn't change: all my buddies got uniforms except me. I can't tell you how much that hurt. I was devastated. Of all the kids there, I felt I was the most committed—the only one who had run laps all summer, thrown the football every day, and was totally focused on trying to make the team. All the rest of the thirteen-year-old kids were chasing girls. I was chasing my dream to someday become a quarterback in the NFL. The coach, obviously unaware that he was screwing up my plans, explained that he was sorry he couldn't assign everybody a uniform. But he wasn't nearly as sorry as I was. The consolation prize: Coach told us it was okay to come out and watch practice if we didn't make the team. If somebody got killed or broke a leg, you might get to wear his uniform. A few days later I finally pulled myself together and straggled out to see just how good these guys were. I was standing there in street clothes, watching the players warm up for practice, eaten up with envy, when a football bounced in front of my feet. It was like dropping candy in front of a four-year-old.

I had to get my hands on that football. As the student manager rushed over to retrieve the ball, I gave him my meanest look and he backed off. I said to a friend next to me, "Come on, let's go over there and play catch." We began to pitch and catch on an adjacent field. Even back in the eighth grade, I could throw the ball fifty-five yards. So I passed it to my friend and glanced over my shoulder to see if any of the coaches were watching. I was afraid that I was going to get in trouble for taking the ball. But I couldn't pass up the chance to show off with the hope of getting discovered. Basically, I was auditioning. Now that I had this football in my hands, I had to act, so I was throwing it as hard and as far as I could.

Suddenly I looked over my shoulder and saw the coach coming in my direction with raised arms. I was so scared I began to run with the ball tucked under my arm. As the coach ran after me, he hollered, "Wait a minute!" I began to cry as I ran. The coach grabbed me by the collar and I really began to weep and wail. "Nononononono!" he said. "It's okay. Where'd you learn to throw the football like that?" I told him I'd been throwing the ball like that since I was in fourth grade. I said it indignantly. I felt like asking him why he hadn't noticed it before now. After all, how would Elvis have responded if they'd asked him where he learned to sing?

We began to walk back toward the dressing room and the coach draped his arm around me and uttered the phrase that would change my life: "Come on, son, we're going to get you a uniform." Bells went off in my head. It was a dream come true: I was going to be a genuine, bona fide football player, a quarterback, a star. He gave me a helmet, jersey, and pads. I'd never worn a helmet that meant so much; I couldn't believe the feeling. I just sat there with that helmet on, like a king wearing his crown, feeling like football royalty. I can still remember the smell of that helmet and that uniform, but I had no idea where the pads were supposed to go or how to put them on. The year before when I had played Pop Warner football, my pads snapped on in my pants, but this was a big-time uniform. I had never put on a jock strap in my life and had no idea if we were supposed to wear it over or under our underwear. I had the right thigh pad upside down in the left leg and was completely befuddled when the coach came to my rescue. None of this was a major concern to me, however, because I was one happy kid. I was a football player with a uniform to prove it.

That night I was bursting with pride to tell my dad. When I didn't come home on the bus, my parents came looking for me. As soon as I saw them I started screaming and hollering with joy. Dad had said the year before, "Hang on and keep trying and something good will happen." He had promised me that if I made the team, he'd buy me some cleats. I couldn't wait another minute. We went down to Sears and picked out a pair. I couldn't have just any old football shoes. Low-cut shoes were still a novelty item and high school players didn't wear white shoes in those days, but I spotted a pair of black ones with some white bird wings on them and white nylon cleats that made clickety-clack sounds when you walked so that people could hear you coming a mile away. I knew that if Dad would only buy them for me, I would be capable of running faster than the speed of sound and would probably become an All-American in a matter of days. I think Dad knew better, but he went along with it and bought them anyway.

The most memorable moment was yet to come. Before I made the team, I would hang around the gym and watch with envy as these other guys paraded out of the dressing room, all decked in pads and gear. When they walked across the concrete basketball court outside the gym, their cleats clickety-clacking, the sound was memorable, a sound that made people snap their heads around to see if maybe thoroughbred horses were walking on a marble floor. Just to hear that sound was exhilarating. The next day, as we left the dressing room and walked across that basketball court, I will never forget the sound of those nylon cleats clickety-clacking on concrete. What beautiful music!

I will always cherish the memory of that first pair of football shoes, which probably cost all of about fifteen dollars. A boy's first pair of football shoes ranks right up there with his first kiss. The Oak Terrace Fighting Trojans had black and red uniforms, the ugliest of any team in Shreveport: plain, no stripe even on the pants—looked like Penn State. But to me, that uniform was more beautiful than any three-piece suit I would ever own.

The coach put me at middle linebacker. A few weeks later I broke my collarbone in two places. Finally, in ninth grade, I became the starting quarterback—my first step on the road to Pittsburgh, thanks to another lucky bounce of a football.

I arrived in Pittsburgh as a rookie so naive about life that I wanted to walk up to people on the street and lick their faces like a big puppy dog. I was scared to death they would discover that I was only little old Terry Bradshaw from Shreveport, Louisiana, who didn't know a zone defense from a zip code.

A flip of a coin had decided my fate this time and not the bounce of a football. Like the Steelers, the Chicago Bears had won only one game that season, and, ironically, that was 38–7 against—do you believe it?—the Steelers. Chuck Noll won his first game as a rookie coach, 16–13, and lost all the rest. So the two teams flipped a coin for the first pick in the 1970 draft. The Steelers won and chose me. The Bears picked tackle Rufus Mayes of Ohio State.

Three seasons after that draft, my dreams and the hopes of generations of sports fans in Pittsburgh converged into one unforgettable magic moment.

Three Rivers was rockin' that famous day in December. Each star player had his own little cult among the fans. There was Gerela's Gorillas, a group of devotees to place-kicker Roy Gerela, some of whom actually wore gorilla costumes. There was Franco's Italian Army, followers of our great running back Franco Harris, who wore combat fatigues long before Rambo made them popular. Franco's Army came to the games with grenades, green berets, machetes, combat boots, and, I swear, I think half of them parachuted into their seats from helicopters. The guards at the back gate even wore combat helmets. Franco was our Italian Stallion, a kind of Rocky Balboa of the Steelers, and if he had chosen to lead his troops to war, I have no doubt they would have followed him straight to Southeast Asia.

Then there was the other Rocky—Rocky Bleier, the Vietnam veteran, the tough little guy with the big heart. Rocky was a star running back, the captain of his Notre Dame team, a brave soldier who had part of his foot shot off in Vietnam. He was a favorite of our owner, Art Rooney, who kept Rocky around on injured reserve and, I believe, paid for the surgery on his foot. Then we had Kolb's Kowboys, the disciples of Jon Kolb, the big offensive tackle from Oklahoma State. And there was Jack Ham, the Polish linebacker from Penn State. Polish people would send him Polish hams.

Mean Joe Greene's fans were in fine form and so were the supporters of Ernie "Fats" Holmes, who was just a rookie. There might even have been a few Terry Bradshaw fans, but not many, because I was still struggling just to keep my starting job. It was an incredible collection of spectators. And they were primed for this stirring moment in Steeler history, what I like to call—with tongue in cheek—"The Immaculate Reception."

The Steelers were coached by Chuck Noll, a little-known assistant from Baltimore who had come to them from Don Shula's staff in 1969. After winning just five and losing nine my rookie season, Noll's team won six and lost eight in 1971, showing little improvement. But the Steelers of 1972 surprised the league by winning nine of their last ten games for an 11–3 record, and the city of Pittsburgh got hotter than the foundry at U.S. Steel. The good people of Pittsburgh were simply not prepared for what they were about to witness. Nor was I.

Trailing 7–6, we were all looking for a miracle in the last seventy-two seconds of our first-round American Football Conference playoff game against the Raiders. Unaccustomed as we were to the circumstances at hand—being in a position to still win but not really knowing what it would take—there was little hope that we could escape what appeared to be inevitable defeat.

The Raiders had put a clamp on our star rookie Harris, who had gained a thousand yards rushing that season, and at the half it was a scoreless tie. Oakland quarterback Daryl Lamonica was suffering from a bout with the flu, so he was replaced in the fourth quarter by a young left-hander named Kenny Stabler. I finally completed a couple of passes and we got two field goals out of Gerela for a 6–0 lead with just under four minutes to play. There probably weren't many fans there that day who believed we could hold on to win against the mighty Raiders. And I guarantee you there was not one who thought we could come back to win it after

Stabler caught us in a safety blitz and scored. George Blanda kicked the extra point to put Oakland ahead by one. There was no chance to return the Raiders' kickoff because Blanda hit the goal posts, which in those days were still on the goal line.

If the Steelers would have told the truth, we would have admitted to being ready to pack up our gear and leave the field, because all of us thought we had already heard the all-too familiar refrain of The Fat Lady. We had no shot. Our offense had been stuffed by the Raiders' defense all day. The chances of our scoring on the Raiders at that point were about as likely as Johnny U. showing up in our huddle, wearing Steeler black and gold again, and asking: "Can I help, guys?" We were an unproven commodity, a young team without an identity or a winning tradition, directed by a quarterback who had always been long on dreams but short on big-time credentials.

The worst sin a football player can commit is to confess he is a realist in the face of trouble. Athletes learn at an early age to ignore the facts at hand and deny the inevitable. You may be scared to death, totally uncertain about the next few seconds of your life, but you don't ever admit it for fear of being branded a quitter, non-believer, and a lousy team player. Here in the last minute of the most important football game played to that date in Pittsburgh, I was glad the Steeler coaching staff didn't ask me to take a loyalty oath, because I would have flunked.

Quarterbacks are supposed to be brash, cocky field generals with tunnel vision and a strong sense of purpose. It's the quarterback's job to inspire the ten other men around him in the huddle, and coaches say if that quarterback wavers just a tiny bit, the team's confidence will erode. I was a little short on confidence at the moment. So I had to fake my coolness. I had my walk down to perfection and could swagger in and out of the huddle like a show horse. As long as the fans didn't see my knees shaking, they probably said: "Look at that Bradshaw boy! He's in total control." I had very little confidence that I could move the Steelers the final eighty yards for the winning touchdown against the Raiders. Fact is, I was just trying to get us a first down.

I was a young quarterback who'd never been in that situation before, never had to carry such a load, and here we were on national TV, playing these mean, nasty, spiteful Raiders, who not only had a Commitment to Excellence, but a Commitment to Kicking Our Butts. They had already played in one Super Bowl and probably viewed this game as a minor inconvenience on their way to the AFC Championship Game.

I had spent most of the day handing the ball off left or handing it off right, with an occasional pass, because that's the kind of offense Noll ran then. I wasn't doing much to help our cause. And although I did get the Steelers up to the forty yard line, two of my next three passes were knocked down by the Raiders' great defensive back Jack Tatum, who was to be a central character in the drama that was soon to unfold.

You can see why my confidence was lacking as we got in the huddle, looking down field at sixty yards of green artificial turf between us and the end zone. So far that day it had been virgin territory to the Steelers, except for Gerela's two field goals.

In the hurry-up offense, or two-minute drill, time can be your best ally or worst enemy. Everything is in high gear. Quarterbacks generally call two plays at a time in the huddle, and it takes a savvy veteran to use the clock exactly right. Unitas was a master at it. You throw an incomplete pass out of bounds to stop the clock, regroup, and call two more plays. We were regrouping in the huddle. Our big tight end from Clemson, John McMakin, had been telling me all day that he could get open and so I fired one off to him, incomplete, and we scampered back to the huddle in search of something else that might work. On the second play, I threw it over the middle to McMakin again, incomplete, almost right into the hands of a Raider. Tatum knocked it away. The first lucky bounce. Time was running out and I was feeling more pressure every second. I tried one more pass to my left, this one to wide receiver Al Young, but Tatum was there again.

It was fourth down and ten with twenty-two seconds to play and Chuck sent in a play. We had not produced a single yard in three tries. I had completed just ten of twenty-four passes for a mere 115 yards. How was I going to complete a fourth down pass against the Oakland Raiders when I had been playing terribly? All of a sudden I was faced with throwing the greatest pass of my life. The fans were scream-ing so loud that I could hardly hear the play Chuck sent in as it was repeated in the huddle. I was supposed to hit Barry Pearson, the receiver from Northwestern in his first season as a Steeler, somewhere over the middle.

It was fourth down with a long, long way to go when I took the snap from Ray Mansfield and dropped back, feeling the heat of the Raider rush like a blowtorch in my face. Oak-land's two defensive ends, Tony Cline and Horace Jones, had arrived in the pocket almost as quickly as I did. Across the field, big John Madden was on a rampage, yelling at his Raiders to play deep in the prevent defense and watch for the long pass.

No matter how tall a quarterback is—and I'm 6'3"—you only feel about 5'6" when you stride and stretch out to throw the football with giant 6'8" defensive linemen coming at you. I felt like a midget as I looked for a crack of daylight, hoping to see a Steeler jersey somewhere in the clear.

The final twenty-two seconds had all but evaporated. I couldn't see Franco, but he was downfield waving and yell-ing for my attention. I thought I saw Frenchy Fuqua over the middle and figured I could throw a deep post route. A huge figure in silver and black was bearing down on me from my left side, so I moved to the right in the pocket. When I cocked my arm, I wasn't sure where I was going to throw the ball because I couldn't see downfield, but I knew the worst thing for me to do was get sacked. One guy was grabbing me; I shook loose and had to push another guy off with my left hand. I was swinging the ball, about to throw, and another

Raider came barreling at me in mid-air, so I ducked and he went flying over my shoulder. When I came up I saw people all around me, and I knew I had to get rid of the ball in a hurry. So I gunned it. And when I gunned it, I got gunned. Knocked flat on my ass.

When you get knocked to the ground on a football field and can't see the action, you listen carefully for telltale sounds. You learn to read those noises the way an Indian reads bear tracks. There's a good roar and a bad roar. I was on my back and couldn't see anything but gray sky overhead, green artificial turf, and black and silver uniforms on top of me. The ball was somewhere on the way toward Fuqua—I thought—because as I unloaded it, I thought I saw a number 33 in the middle of the field. So I turned up my hearing to listen for a clue as to what had happened.

Of all the roars I have ever heard, there's never been one to compare to that one. As I picked my head up off the turf, knowing instinctively that all but a few seconds had expired on the game clock, I had the feeling something wonderful had happened. The fans were going nuts. And as I jumped up, I saw something truly miraculous: Franco crossing the goal line and going into the end zone. Art Rooney, Sr., had left the owner's box before the end of the game, thinking we had lost, and was waiting in the dressing room to console us. He heard the unexpected noise and asked an attendant what had happened. Stunned, Mr. Rooney couldn't believe the news. The attendant told him to listen to the crowd noise—it was a good roar.

Fans streamed onto the field, some of them mobbing me. I realized we had won, but I still didn't know how. "This is unbelievable! Unbelievable!" I said. "Somebody tell me. What happened?" They just kept hollering, "You did it, you did it!" And I kept asking, "Did what? Somebody please tell me!"

Then I got a grip on myself and said, "Terry, you quarterbacking demon! You must have threaded the needle right in there amongst all those Oakland Raiders and hit Frenchy

and then he lateralled to Franco who went in for a touchdown." I started feeling pretty good about myself. And I
knew it was time to get my quotes down. As a pro athlete you
learn early to get your quotes down. When you talk to the
press after a big play or big game, you need to sound a little
bit hip, throwing in a few technical terms so that they never
totally understand what you're saying. And always act hum-
ble while taking credit for something that you really don't
deserve.

You'll still get different opinions from each side about
what actually happened on The Immaculate Reception.
Here's the Steelers' version: Tatum of the Raiders, going up
for the ball at the same time as Fuqua at the Oakland thirty-
five yard line, knocked it back in my direction about twenty
feet as he collided with Frenchy. The ball caromed toward
Franco, who was standing at about the Raiders' forty-two
yard line, hoping to get my attention. Franco had taken off
running toward Frenchy after seeing the ball was thrown to
him, looking to throw a block. Harris later said that as he
ran toward Frenchy, he saw the ball pop out. "The ball kept
coming straight at me," he said, "and from there it was all
instinct." Franco reached down below his knees for the ball
and I swear it was no higher than a half-inch off the artificial surface. He took off running with Jim Warren of the
Raiders chasing him and scored with five seconds left in the
game.

Speaking as an observer of game films and not an eye
witness—I was only an "earwitness"—I think the ball must
have been hit first by Tatum, the defender. Coming from his
defensive backfield position, Tatum knocked the ball backward toward me. I don't believe I threw the ball hard enough
for it to hit Frenchy and bounce backward twenty feet to the
spot where Harris made the catch. If it had hit Frenchy in
the chest at the angle he was running, the football would
have veered off to the right instead of straight backwards,
because of the ricochet factor. See what I mean? Frenchy is
moving laterally across the field, Tatum is coming from his
safety position, they converge on the ball, and Tatum's mo-

mentum carries the ball backward. There has never been conclusive evidence as to whether it hit Tatum or Fuqua first. All we can do is speculate. It may have hit them at exactly the same time.

You can understand why Raider fans still get emotional about this call, because if it was wrong, their team might have been screwed out of going to the Super Bowl that year. If Frenchy *did* touch the ball first, then the play was voided. In those days, it was illegal for a ball to be touched first by another offensive player, as the Raiders claim Fuqua did, before being caught. Frenchy has said in past years that he didn't, but now when you ask him he likes to play coy. The only people who really know for sure are Frenchy and Tatum. I never see or hear from Jack and don't expect to. Frenchy, who now works in the *Detroit News* circulation department, doesn't want to say and is either going to take his secret to the grave or write a book about it himself someday.

I'm not even sure Frenchy could settle the argument anyway, because nobody is ever going to convince those irate Raider fans that we won fair and square. So we can forget that. However, we shouldn't let that controversy taint the historical significance of The Immaculate Reception or diminish Franco's great effort—he pulled off a spectacular catch. No matter how many times experts looked at tape and film, they could never really get the real truth. Even the still photos of Franco clutching the ball just above the artificial turf were slightly blurry, so you couldn't see for sure if he had possession—although there's no question that he did. Twilight Zone stuff, man.

There was no such thing as use of instant replay by the officials back in 1972, although the networks were using it in their telecasts. Madden reminded me one day years later that referee Fred Swearingen did not signal for a touchdown right away. First, he went to the sideline and conferred by phone with Art McNally, chief of NFL officials, in the press box. Swearingen's crew didn't know who touched the ball first, so they had ruled it was touched simultaneously and

wanted to know if there was anything revealing in the replay. They even rigged up a special TV for Swearingen on
the sideline so he could watch the replay at the same time.
McNally concurred: no conclusive evidence to reverse the
call. This was the first time in NFL history that TV was used
to aid an official's judgment. Instant replay was born.

I don't think Madden will ever forgive us for winning that
game, especially the unorthodox way we did it. He was
stomping along the sidelines, trying to figure out what happened like everyone else. And Madden would never let his
team forget the bitter defeat, which set the stage for the
great Steelers-Raiders rivalry in years to come. We paid for
our good fortune: the next season the Raiders whipped our
tails, 33–14, in the AFC playoffs. But over the next four
seasons it was pretty even: the Raiders and Steelers met in
four straight postseason contests, with each team winning
two games.

So many lives were affected by what happened in Pittsburgh on December 23, 1972. The seeds of the Steelers'
dynasty years were planted right there in the artificial turf
of Three Rivers Stadium when the football took such an
incredibly bountiful bounce for us. Some men went on to
become famous and a few even made small fortunes. Nobody benefited from it more than Chuck Noll, who was still
there long after the dynasty years ended, picking up the
pieces.

2
CHUCK

I can still see those hands: fingernails always well-mani-cured and clean. Wedding band on his ring finger. Chuck Noll's hands represented control, and he always seemed to have them strategically locked onto a jersey or an arm or a face mask, just to make his point. You could feel the anger in his grip. I got to where I couldn't stand for Chuck to put his hands on me. When I was a rookie, Chuck jerked me around on the sidelines during the games. Against the Giants my second year, he grabbed me by the face mask in front of teammates, dragged me around like an animal, and screamed at me. It was humiliating.

So Chuck and I have experienced some rocky times to-gether and I've made my feelings known about him publicly many times before. In the three years of working on this book, I've run the gamut on my feelings about my former coach, from anger to confusion to gratitude. That's why this particular chapter has been written and rewritten about a half-dozen times. I would only ask that you hear me out all the way through, this one last time, on what I am about to say about Chuck Noll.

As the years progressed and we won some Super Bowls, you could almost detect how much Chuck's esteem for me had grown just by the way he placed his hands on me. He was more gentle. He would put his arm around my waist on the sidelines while we were conferring on a play. Sometimes he would put his hand on my shoulder pad. But Chuck didn't jerk me around anymore, never grabbed me by the face mask. His hands expressed gratitude and respect.

When my confidence evolved and I became more independent, as eventually happens to all quarterbacks who survive and start, Chuck would latch on to my jersey—gently—to keep me at his side, because he knew if he didn't keep a firm hand on me, I'd run back to the huddle and call my own play.

You look at the hands, then trace the arms up to the face until you meet those eyes. Most people's eyes reflect an emotion like happiness, sadness, or surprise. When you look into Chuck Noll's eyes, you see nothing. They appear mysterious—cold and emotionless.

It's tragic that Chuck and I had such a stormy relationship. Sometimes I wonder if he really ever wanted to draft me; I have this theory that he was forced by somebody else in the Steelers organization to take me as the number-one pick, because he never gave me any reason to think differently. That must have influenced our relationship. Maybe he didn't like me. He knew I was a southern kid. That I didn't know how to read defenses. That I was a long-term project.

People have questioned whether Chuck ever knew how to handle quarterbacks, which may have been the reason he hired Babe Parilli as quarterback coach in my second year. After all, Chuck was a messenger guard with the Cleveland Browns team and never really understood a quarterback's mentality. I was a young quarterback struggling with both my professional and personal life and was totally confounded by what appeared to be Chuck's indifference. In fact, I never felt Chuck liked me and took the quirks in his personality as a testimony to his displeasure with me.

Shortly after my retirement I was doing a CBS telecast of a

game in which the Steelers were playing at the Orange Bowl. Before the game, Chuck passed me on the field and just stared at me. He just snapped his fingers and walked right by, completely ignoring me. I know that he saw me; it was devastating to have your coach of more than fourteen years act as though you were invisible. I looked him right in the eyes—as always, they were empty—hoping that he'd come over and shake my hand. He didn't. We had shared so much together, climbing to the top of the mountain, laughing together, singing together as he strummed my guitar in training camp. And now the man didn't have time to even acknowledge my existence. To this day I don't know why he did that, but perhaps somewhere along the way I said or did something that caused him to feel hostile. Still, his snub hurt me.

Our differences began early on. My rookie year under Chuck was almost like fraternity hazing. He confused me—yanking me out of games in the first quarter, moving me up and down the depth chart. And it seemed as though he never missed a chance to make an example out of me.

I was late for a team meal in Houston once when Art Rooney, Jr., stopped me to offer some words of encouragement because he knew I was struggling in my first year. Rooney was simply assuring me of my future. Since I was standing just outside the door, in full view, Chuck could see who I was talking to, but he chose to make a spectacle out of my being a few minutes tardy. It was no big deal being a couple of minutes late because players were always dragging in from chapel or just not arriving on time. But Chuck chose this time to crack down on punctuality. When I walked in, he stood up and said, "Miisssssstter Braaadshaw! You're late and that's going to cost you a hundred bucks!" Humiliated me right in front of my teammates before a game. Why would you want to put down your starting quarterback like that? I was a rookie and certainly didn't want to cause any problems. Then to rub it in, he started me, played me in the first quarter, and brought in Terry Hanratty in the second period. I couldn't understand what coach in his right mind would want to belittle a young player that way. I was emotionally distraught.

Perhaps some of my immature actions aggravated him—like stopping over in Louisiana after a game to visit my parents and returning to Pittsburgh late. I was headed back for practice on a Tuesday when I got fogged in at the St. Louis airport. When I realized I couldn't get there on time, I phoned Chuck to inform him. He seemed perfectly agreeable, and although I could detect a tiny bit of hostility in his voice, I took that to mean I had been granted permission. But I had no idea he was going to explode when I arrived in Pittsburgh. All I had missed was a film session and some light running. I arrived later that day, but the following day he made me stand up in a team meeting and announced that he was going to fine me. Unloaded on me. We had won our game, beaten Houston, and instead of coming back as a hero, I felt I was being scolded like a child. Here I'd been fined twice already and you can understand why I was walking around saying, "Get me out of here and away from this madman!" From my own selfish standpoint, it seemed he went out of his way to hurt me. So let's look at it from Chuck's perspective. There's some psychology here and what is it? Well, if you're late, you're "not committed." And if you stay home, you're immature and you're not concentrating on football—you're more worried about being around your family than your teammates. Again, Chuck had to have control.

Admittedly, part of the problem was my naivete about pro football as a business. To me it had always been a game; I was out to have fun, win, and, as always, get along with my coaches, whom I had always held in the utmost respect. Still, this was not the way you would expect one of the so-called coaching legends to handle his starting quarterback. If Chuck was trying to make an impression on me, he accomplished it, because it has taken me twenty years to finally put it in perspective.

Looking back on it now, it saddens me that I never had any kind of postcareer relationship with the Steelers organization. The separation process started in my final season, 1983, when Chuck began making caustic comments about my career being over and suggesting that my value to the Steelers was virtually nothing. I was injured and Chuck discouraged me from being around the team while I was recuperating from elbow surgery. Had Chuck asked me to come to the games and stand on the sidelines, I would gladly have done so, but I didn't receive any indication that I was wanted, or needed. I wasn't told *not* to attend the games—I just didn't think I was welcome there. And Chuck made it known to the media that he'd just as soon not have me around.

While I was injured that year, the Steelers were beaten 17–14 by the Minnesota Vikings on November 20 and Chuck was asked by the Pittsburgh media if I was ever going to return to the team. A writer from the *Pittsburgh Press*, Ron Cook, called me in Grand Cane, Louisiana, to tell me how Chuck responded when asked about my possible return. Chuck told them: "I don't know if he can throw or not. Maybe he's ready for his life's work."

Everybody knew what Chuck was saying, although he had never said it to me. Bob Smizik of the *Press* wrote: "That's Noll's way of saying maybe Bradshaw should retire from football." Retire? I wasn't one of those jocks who was going to hang on until they ripped my uniform off. I thought I was ready for the real world, but I hadn't gone through elbow surgery just for the fun of it and had hoped to play five more years until I was forty. That my coach had other ideas came as a bit of a shock. Chuck wouldn't tell me he thought I should quit, but he also wouldn't give me the satisfaction of feeling needed. I wanted so badly for him to express something about my contributions to the team or call me aside and tell me that it was painful for him after all we had been through together, but that maybe it was time for me to go on down the road. I wondered why he couldn't have just shaken my hand, thanked me for helping his teams win four Super Bowls, and said good-bye. Maybe I could have dealt with that. Instead, it seemed Chuck was dropping hints in the newspapers that I ought to be looking for another line of work. Again, I was hurt and mixed up.

Pretty soon I began to strike back in the press. But shooting off my mouth was a mistake—all we did was trade sarcastic remarks. The reason I responded in anger wasn't just because of the way Chuck treated me; I began to feel as though he had no appreciation for what our team had accomplished together. Later, when Franco Harris was holding out during training camp, the press asked Chuck about Franco. He smirked and said, "Franco who?"

Yes, I know pro football is a business, but I always played the game primarily for fun, although it was my main source of income. I never held out or complained about my salary. Hey, they were paying me to do something that I dearly loved. I always tried to keep in mind that football is still a game. And I did have fun. There were times when I even had fun with Chuck. It's hard to believe now, but we actually got along on occasion. It seemed as though the good times were only there for as long as I could play quarterback and the Steelers could win, but deep down I was hoping he cared for me as a person.

Looking back now at the Steelers' accomplishments, my wish is that someday we can all enjoy them together. What the Steelers did in the mid '70s will probably never be duplicated—at least not in our lifetimes. I'm not stupid enough to say that the players did it by themselves: Chuck will surely go down as one of the best coaches in NFL history. It's too bad, though, that Chuck and I became estranged. We spent so much time together as quarterback and coach and I took that to mean that we were friends, yet the friendship ended when I was no longer of any use to Chuck. Or at least that's how it seemed.

When the whole world was calling me "dumb" and people referred to me as Li'l Abner and Ozark Ike, I needed Chuck and he wasn't there. When I was injured late in my career and was feeling insecure, unwanted, and unneeded, as all injured football players do, I felt Chuck was turning his back on me. Yet back when I was in training camp, Chuck would come down to my room and pick up my guitar, strum a few bars of a folk song, and then try to convince me I could play with my injury. That was when my right elbow was mush.

When the end came, I needed Chuck most of all and he wasn't there. I remember the day in the weight room when I told him, "I can't play anymore, Chuck." He just sat there staring at me with those cold, unfeeling eyes, not saying a word. I shook his hand—the last time I would ever have to deal with his hands again as a player—and he shook his head as I walked away.

People often ask me about what coaches I admire. I wouldn't be foolish enough to exclude Chuck from the list because he has enjoyed great success. I separate my favorite coaches into categories—some because of my personal relationships with them, some because of their coaching genius, and some because of their organization. My personal favorite was Bum Phillips, of the Houston Oilers, who had a big heart and was a loving, caring person to everybody. He was also a winning coach who captured the imagination of the public and the attention of the players. I would have loved to play for him because of the respect he showed for his players. Bill Walsh of the Forty-Niners and Joe Gibbs of the Redskins both have brilliant offensive minds. Then if you mix in the discipline and teaching ability of Don Shula of the Dolphins, plus a touch of the Cowboys' Tom Landry's offensive and defensive trickery, you'd have the perfect coach, as far as I'm concerned. I would have to include Chuck's organizational skills, his eye for detail, and his ability to recognize talent.

If you put the traits of all those coaches into one man and let him work for Al Davis of the Raiders, I'd love to have the chance to play for him until I was fifty years old. I always admired the way Davis took care of his players, even after they left the game. That isn't to say I would trade Mr. Rooney for a hundred Al Davises, but I admired his style.

As rigid as he was, Chuck always relied on his players to play the game. He drafted them, coached them, and prepared them, but they had to perform for him on the field. Unlike Paul Brown, one of his mentors, Chuck let his quarterbacks call their own plays. And the game plan never changed. We may have had 150 plays, but I always narrowed it down to about forty. I was so enamored of Chuck's intelligence back in those days that I believed with all my heart that this was the perfect game plan, even though it was the same game plan we had the week before. And sometimes it *was* perfect.

You may have a hard time believing this, but the game plan I used in Super Bowl IX when we beat Minnesota was the same one, with only slight variations, that we had when we beat the Rams in Super Bowl XIV five years later. The philosophy of the offense was pretty much the same: run trap plays and throw deep. On defense we blitzed a little bit more, but we still believed in playing aggressively, stuffing the run, and forcing the opponent to throw. In those days, defensive philosophy was shifting toward the three-man front, but we stuck with the stunt four-three. As far as I know, Chuck, maybe with the help of George Perles, was the innovator of the stunt four-three, where Joe Greene was slanted toward the center, forcing two or three offensive linemen to block one man, thereby freeing middle linebacker Jack Lambert.

Chuck was never a motivator and he didn't believe in fiery pregame or halftime speeches. But I will always remember one comment he made in 1974 prior to the game against the Raiders for the American Football Conference Championship on the way to our first Super Bowl. He said, simply and directly: "People don't give us a chance, but we are going to go out there and beat those SOBs!" The room erupted with a big cheer and I thought it was the greatest thing I'd ever heard. We beat them 24–13 on their home field.

I will say this much for Noll as a coach: he knew every tiny detail about his football team, from what we were trying to do on defense to the wide receivers' blocking routes on offense. Until I went to work for CBS and began to meet other head coaches in the NFL, I thought that was the way all head coaches were. But a lot of head coaches handle only the offense, or only the defense, and in some cases only the management of the team and the media. Noll is a rare species in today's modern world of specialization.

That's not to say Chuck was terribly creative with his offense; we weren't a fancy team. But he knew what the running backs were supposed to do, all the adjustments, all the audibles and the calls by the offensive linemen, what the linebackers, defensive lineman, the safeties, and corners were supposed to do. He knew the total package, right down to the special teams. Unlike many NFL coaches, who spend most of their time making speeches and talking to the press, Chuck Noll coached. The man has great pride and a huge ego. There was no doubt that this was Chuck Noll's football team: he wanted everybody to know that but didn't want to be too obvious about it. He thrived on it when his starting quarterback was injured and he won with Cliff Stoudt, or when he won without Joe Greene. He loves it when people say the Steelers get the credit and he stands in the background.

The smartest thing Chuck ever did was go out and hire Parilli in my second season. Babe was my saving grace for a couple of years. He may have been the first quarterback coach in the NFL. I blossomed under Babe because he treated me like a man, he stroked me and built up my confidence. Babe was great.

"Chuck's strength was that he had total control of the team," Babe told me. "Everybody was always on time. Players and coaches alike were disciplined. But as far as offense went, Chuck had a lot to learn."

Chuck knew what he wanted to do and didn't want to be bothered by any dissenting views. That's probably why he always brought in young coaches and taught them his way. He wanted their fresh ideas, but he wanted to school them in the Chuck Noll way. He taught Perles, whose Michigan State team won the Big Ten title in 1987 and the 1988 Rose Bowl. He taught Woody Widenhofer, now with the Detroit Lions, who coached the Steeler linebackers before he went to Missouri as head coach. And Chuck taught Lionel Taylor, then his wide receiver coach. He taught Tom Moore, who's still his offensive coordinator, and Dick Hoak, who coaches the backfield.

There were a few exceptions: Bud Carson, the new head coach of the Cleveland Browns, former defensive coordinator for the Jets and the man generally credited as author of the Steel Curtain defense, brought his own philosophy, although I'm sure Chuck influenced it heavily. And Dan Radokovich brought in the pushing technique for offensive linemen, which proved to be revolutionary because the linemen could keep their feet, jam with their open-palm hands, attack, and recoil. That kind of pass-blocking technique gave me an extra half-second. We were the first team to do that. In the end, though, it had to be Chuck's system, because he wanted his stamp on everything. Sometimes we could hear an assistant coach arguing with Chuck, but normally a strong-willed person doesn't stay around long.

Chuck is a paradox to many people because he's so unlike other NFL coaches. He never wrote a book. He didn't do TV commercials. He never had any kind of TV show, let alone one the magnitude of a Mike Ditka, a Bill Parcells, or a Dan Reeves. He didn't own a restaurant. And he's basically publicity shy. He hates crowds; they make him uncomfortable. Chuck is only comfortable when he's in total control; I suspect that's why he always thinks he has to become an expert on everything he does. He knows all about classical music and fine wine. He knows about politics, of course. You want to talk about coffee, Chuck can smell coffee beans and try to discern whether they are from Colombia or Mexico or Brazil or the Canary Islands. Want to talk about weather? He knows everything about thunderstorms, snow, lightning, rain, sleet, or hail. Want to discuss grass? He can talk about agronomy—or Deuteronomy. His best friend was a pilot, so Chuck became a pilot. He started playing golf and couldn't master it, so he gave it up for a while. He had to have complete control of everything. At just about everything else he tried, he was one of the world's leading experts. Just ask him. He certainly wasn't shy about letting you know what he knew, either.

It took vision to assemble the Steelers of the '70s. I don't know whether it was Chuck's genius or the genius of his scouts. He didn't trade for us; he built through the draft. He looked around and saw the success Don Shula was having in Miami with Larry Csonka, so he went out and got a big back—Franco Harris. We were the first team to start throwing the football all over the field. That's because Chuck went out and got a quarterback and a couple of great receivers named Lynn Swann and John Stallworth, not to mention Randy Grossman and Benny Cunningham. Ever so slowly, the pieces began to fit together.

Chuck always has had a master plan but doesn't always have the players to make it work. The problem today is that Chuck Noll no longer has the players and has never been flexible enough to adapt. It also puzzles me that he won't go out and hire a brilliant offensive coordinator or at least turn Tom Moore loose to make some changes.

Chuck's biggest shortcoming in the '80s is probably a lack of drive. Like everyone else who's had success, it was tough for him to stay hungry, although I do think he has been working hard again recently to pull the Steelers together. That's probably true of most coaches who have been head man for more than a decade. I'm sure Chuck, Tom Landry, and Don Shula felt they were working harder than ever during the 1988 season, but all had losing records and I don't think defeat stung them the way it used to. In the case of Landry, the change of ownership in Dallas and his lack of success in rebuilding the Cowboys resulted in his dismissal. In my later years, when Chuck began to mellow, I'd see him laughing to himself on the sideline when we were getting our tails beat, although it may have been out of frustration.

The only real positive steps I've seen Chuck take in recent years were bringing ex-Steelers Joe Greene and Jon Kolb back as assistant coaches (Kolb was later named strength coach). I like Kolb; I love Joe Greene and have a lot of faith in him. But I hope Kolb and Greene aren't too little too late:

Chuck just hasn't adjusted to the times on offense. Bubby Brister showed promise before he was hurt in 1988, but it didn't take Bubby long to realize the limitations of Chuck's offense. He commented that perhaps the Steelers "ought to punt on first down"—a remark that got him summoned to Chuck's office. Bubby touched on part of the problem: the lack of offensive imagination. The Steelers did open up a little bit at times in the second half of the season, but their offensive weaponry is not very explosive. Aside from Brister, the last real impact player on offense Chuck drafted was Louis Lipps, the brilliant wide receiver.

The Steelers' curse since their 10–6 record in 1983 was finishing in the middle and drafting fourteenth or fifteenth, where you rarely find any great athletes, instead of getting one of the top five picks. As they were wrapping up the 1988 season on their way to yet another sub-.500 season, there was speculation about whether Chuck was going to survive. Surprisingly, even Steelers president Dan Rooney expressed dissatisfaction with Chuck and his staff for calling "stupid plays" on offense, although Dan also said back when the Steelers had only won two of twelve games that he had no plans to fire Noll. After the Steelers lost to Cleveland 27–7, Dan criticized Chuck for a punt on fourth down and one at the Browns' forty-four yard line. That was a first: I don't recall Dan Rooney ever doing anything but defending Chuck publicly. What happened to Chuck is that he finally became mortal and, like the rest of us, accountable for his failures. He is no longer exempt. That must be a frightening thought to him, as it is to the rest of us when we reach the realization that when we can no longer produce anymore, we become vulnerable and therefore expendable. Ask Tom Landry.

It's almost unbelievable that Chuck is being attacked—the man did win four Super Bowls. Yet if you look at it another way, no coach in the NFL has lost more games during the '80s than Noll. The loss to Cleveland that drew the ire of Rooney turned out to be the seventieth defeat for Chuck in the last nine seasons. Incredibly, this is the same man who won 113 games in the '70s.

To give you an idea of how far the Steelers have sunk, not

even Tom Landry had that many losses—he had fewer than sixty defeats in the '80s—and the general impression is that the Cowboys have been worse off than the Steelers. Pittsburgh's records from 1984 to 1988 were 9-7, 7-9, 6-10, 8-7, and 5-11: an overall record of 35-44. You have to be a pretty successful coach to survive numbers like that.

There was a time when The Quarterback and The Coach were tight. I got along with Chuck so well at one point that the other players used to call him my "daddy." They'd say to me, "Go and ask your daddy if we can work out in shorts today." So I'd go in and talk to Chuck. Most of the time he'd grant the request. But sometimes I'd trick them into thinking my influence was greater than it was. If Chuck had already planned to work out in shorts, I'd walk back in the locker room and say, "Don't worry, fellas, it's all taken care of." They'd say, "Hey, great, Brad! You talked your daddy into it!" I'd say, "You guys just let me know when you need something and I'll take care of it for you." Come Sunday when we were in crunch time, I'd remind the guys: "Hey, fellas, remember last Thursday when I did you a favor with Chuck? Well, I need a little payback. You're going to have to bear down for me on this one." I was everybody's hero and they never caught on to my con game of taking undue credit.

But Chuck's personality kept me off balance, which is probably what he wanted. One minute I was his prodigal son, the next minute I was his dog and he was kicking me. Maybe it was his way of keeping control.

My first few years, I thought everything Chuck said was carved in stone. Over the years, I finally got to a point where I wouldn't pay as much attention to what he said. I would pretend I heard his every word. I'd be looking right in his face as he was talking and he'd be saying something to me that made absolutely no sense. I'd be saying to myself, "You don't even have any idea what you're saying." I'd cuss him out in my mind while he was talking to me. The only times I got in trouble were when he asked me to repeat what he had said.

The most graphic example of my insubordination came in

a game where I had just driven the team ninety-six yards calling my own plays, converting third down and long and third down and short, play-action passes on first down, scrambling for the first down. I knew we were hot: as we moved the ball downfield, our teammates on the sideline were moving with us. Then Chuck signaled for a time out when we were on the other team's two-yard line. I mean, I'm good for ninety-six yards, but I'm not good for the last two, right? But we're really smokin' and somebody hollers, "Brad! Chuck wants you over on the sideline." I turned around, and there he was with his hands in a "T." I thought he wanted to tell me what a fine job I was doing, so I scooted on over to the sideline with my chin strap unsnapped, supremely confident that we were going to score and win this game.

As I have said, I never did like another man putting his hands on me. The first thing Chuck did was grab my jersey. He was trying to get my attention about this play he wanted to call. I pulled away and said to him: "Give me the play!" His mind was upstairs as he listened on his headset to the assistant coaches, getting the scoop on this great play, and I was running out of patience, something I never have been long on anyway. So I pulled loose and began trotting back on the field. The official had started the clock and I was standing there on the field like a fool, because we were about to be penalized for delay of game. Chuck was really steamed at me and began screaming. When Chuck screams he drops his hands to his sides, makes fists, scrunches up his face like a baby ready to cry, and gets real red. That's how he looked. So I said, "I'd better get on back over there, because Chuck has got this play." Back to the sideline I go and now Chuck has his hands on me again, holding me by the jersey.

"What is the play?" I hollered at him, but he just kept on talking. Time was running out, the ref was lining things up, and by now it is time to get on with it. So I took Chuck's hands and pushed them away, turned around and ran back in the game as he was yelling at me to come back. I hollered an obscenity at him over my shoulder, went back in the huddle, called my own play, ran a sprint-right pick, and we scored the winning touchdown. When I came off the field he was smiling.

I had just leveled my head coach, the way he used to level me, for all teammates to see. Now I had to go and face the music. Much to my surprise, the man was very pleased. But from then on, I knew I had gotten the upper hand on him—I threatened him and he backed off. He'd bluffed me for all those years and now in the 1977 season I had finally had enough. I had him. King check.

He is a typical head coach who bullies his players, and I had let him get away with it until then. But eventually a quarterback has to take control of his team, even if it means doing battle with the head coach. Chuck never held that against me. I think he kind of liked it. For me, it was like being a free man—free from the grip of those hands.

I always got a kick out of how he used to tell us that he never read the newspapers in Pittsburgh and that we shouldn't worry about what people write. He thought sportswriters were scumbags, and he sniped at the press in the team meetings every time he got a chance. He'd swear, "I never read that garbage," and then you'd walk into his office and he's reading every newspaper and every magazine article that we all read. It probably miffed Chuck that he couldn't control the writers, too, although he was able to intimidate some of them. In Pittsburgh, you don't read much criticism of Chuck Noll, but writers like Smizik of the *Press* and Phil Musick of the *Post-Gazette* occasionally gave him a body slam.

It was Smizik who challenged Chuck's treatment of me in my final season. He wrote in the *Press*: "It is a strange story that has left Bradshaw almost a player without a team. It has to do with the relationship between Bradshaw and Coach Chuck Noll.... There have been times when the two, to use a favorite expression of Noll's, 'have not been on the same page.' Early on in his career when Bradshaw struggled and later when he was replaced by Joe Gilliam, the relationship sometimes floundered. Even during the championship years they were occasionally a paragraph or two apart. Today, however, they are not even in the same book. Maybe not even in the same library.

"Twice this football season, Chuck Noll has, inexplicably, made statements that had to cut Terry Bradshaw to the bone. They were statements that he had no need to make and that he was not pressed to make, but which he made anyhow."

Those statements, of course, were the ones Chuck made about me "getting on with his life's work" toward the end of my career and "if he can't play quarterback for us, he's no use to us." The notion that Chuck treated me unfairly was at least shared by one other person.

As I was preparing to come back from my injury in 1983 for one last fling, Chuck almost winced at the possibility of having a quarterback controversy. And when it became public knowledge that I was to start against the Jets, which turned out to be my final game, the Pittsburgh media began raising the possibility of a Bradshaw vs. Cliff Stoudt battle, much to Chuck's chagrin. Some even predicted what would happen if I went in the game for Cliff, who had been the starter until then.

Musick wrote the week before my final game: "And, here, a scenario if you will. Saturday afternoon in New York . . . the Jets beating the whey out of a Steelers team mounting the sort of offense usually associated with the Grenadian infantry . . . Stoudt struggling . . . late second quarter. Enter T. Bradshaw on the white charger."

Those kinds of images die hard. I knew I couldn't play anymore after the Jets game, even though I did start and threw two touchdown passes before my arm gave out. Although it was the end, neither Chuck nor I would come out and say it.

I once asked Chuck to trade me. He told me how great I was—and I wasn't even playing. He was doing everything he could to hand the starting quarterback's job to Joe Gilliam, yet when other teams expressed interest, he didn't want to trade me. At the end of my career, he told the press it was time to put me out to pasture. Maybe I should have gotten on with my life's work, but I didn't. I came in as a "dummy" and fought through that image with no help from him. He didn't defend me, or come to my rescue, and, in fact, only contributed to my misery by benching me in favor of Gilliam.

And yet, now that I look back on everything, I have a brutally frank confession to make, one that is going to shock many people who have heard and read my critical comments about Chuck in the five years since my retirement. Chuck Noll was right in the way he handled me, because it made me a better quarterback. I've always responded best to adverse conditions and Chuck was probably smarter than I gave him credit for being. He knew how to bring out the best in me as a football player, although I always felt he didn't understand me as a person.

I think one of the problems Chuck had with me was that he had been around Johnny Unitas as an assistant coach at Baltimore and that was the standard by which I was judged. I have no idea how Johnny Unitas prepared for a game, but evidently he did quite a bit of film study and preparation. I wasn't a guy who liked studying. I just didn't understand why so much emphasis was placed on all this watching of game films because as a college player I'd never had to do that and it was hard for me to change. Chuck always wanted me to look at film, to analyze the defensive formations, but all I wanted to watch was the quarterbacks. You see so many strong-safety rotations, you figure you've seen them all.

There are guys who actually study films so intensely that they take reels home with them. Sometimes they just take film home to impress everyone, hoping the coach will say, "Boy, he sure studies hard." You can create an image like that, so what I did to make Chuck happy was take a lot of film home and just leave it in the trunk of my car. I wasn't about to go home and watch film because that was like taking your job with you after hours. On the other hand, there was a guy named Bob Leahy, from Emporia State, who was constantly watching film. I always wondered what he was looking at. Chuck would call me in and say, "Why don't you study like Bob?" In other words, "Be a little bit of Bob Leahy, be a little bit of Terry Hanratty, be a little bit of

Johnny Unitas." You can look at coverages and say, "I know what a cover-three is," but knowing where to throw the football when you are faced with it is quite another matter. Chuck wanted me to instantly recognize those coverages and to know right away where my receiver was going to be.

I'm sure I was a very frustrating student for Chuck, because I was none of those guys; I was me—and "me" didn't like to study. I wanted to go out to the practice field, throw the football around, and have a grand old time.

I couldn't comprehend the importance of what Chuck was saying, but now I know: grow up, take responsibility, show maturity, apply yourself to your craft, and become a complete quarterback. Chuck knew I had gotten by on pure talent all of my football career and one day I was going to need more than that in the NFL if I was going to be successful. Talent alone wasn't going to get me by anymore, he was saying, and I had to know how to use my ability. Eventually I found out Chuck was right.

I didn't understand exactly what was expected of me. Chuck was trying to tell me, but for whatever reasons, I couldn't hear him. We fought a lot and in my rookie year I hated his guts. The difference is that now I can put myself in Chuck's shoes and can sense what it must be like talking to this kid who has all this talent but absolutely refuses to do the things that will help him develop. I think he probably brought in Parilli as quarterback coach because he was so frustrated with me. So we were both angry.

It turned out that I used my anger to fight back at a time when my career was in jeopardy, because there was always another obstacle, always something to fight off for the starting job. For the first five years our starting quarterbacks were like revolving doors. Gilliam, Hanratty, and I seemed to take turns as the starter. Even Chuck used to say, "One of our quarterbacks has got to take the bull by the horns." He was looking for a leader to come forward.

By challenging me, Chuck made me fight for it, and I wasn't going to let him win. As it turned out, he wasn't trying to win. He just wanted me to grow up, because at twenty-five I was very immature. Those first five hard years forced me to face reality and gave me the confidence in myself for the seasons to come. So when the difficult times hit, when Chuck was jumping on me in the newspapers, it didn't bother me anymore. I may have complained about how Chuck treated me, but I must also give him credit for toughening my hide.

After five long years of fighting with Chuck, I sat down and thought a long time about our relationship. I said to myself, "Here you are talking about this guy, everybody is calling you, quoting you about Chuck, you're talking about him not showing you any respect, and you're telling everybody you're not bitter." But you know what? I *was* bitter. Not bitter that I couldn't play football, because I was ready to move on at the time. I guess what I wanted Chuck to do was say, "There will never be another Terry Bradshaw, what a great young man he is, what a thrill for this football team to have him as a quarterback." I guess I wanted him to stroke my ego, to build me up so that I could feel good about myself.

I'm kind of saddened by it all, how Chuck and I have gone our separate ways, how the Steelers of the '70s are broken up now and we never get together anymore. I wish it all had never happened the way it did. I look back on it and say, "What could I possibly complain about?" We've all had struggles along the way and, unfortunately, many of mine have been documented on the sports pages. I've benefited greatly from the hard bark I developed while playing football and much of that was a result of Chuck's refusing to coddle me. When I talk to sales groups around the country, I often tell them about how I became a stronger person for dealing with adversity. I tell them how Chuck grabbed me by the face mask, how I got knocked down on my butt and fought my way back, how I wasn't going to let him win. But you know what? I realize now that he wanted me to win, because if I won, he had him a quarterback.

I finally see what he was trying to do and I'm grateful for it now. Chuck may have chosen the wrong words when he said, "Maybe it's time for Terry to get on with his life's work." I read that in the paper and it hurt, so I fought back in print.

It was an ugly public fight that neither of us could win. I truly regret all the trash that I brought out, even though I meant it when I said it and don't deny saying it. But now that I look back on it I can see that Chuck was not the kind of person who would know how to deal with my feelings. He's not a guy who passes out compliments, and I knew that. It didn't bother me as a player, so why should it bother me now?

Believe me, I take no great pride in being Chuck Noll's critic. As a matter of fact, I made a promise to myself as I was completing the writing of this book that I'm going to stop criticizing him because it serves no purpose. To be perfectly honest, I've always had a soft spot in my heart for Chuck. He could make me so mad that I hated him. I wanted to choke him. At the same time, while I was still playing and we were trading public insults, I would go into his office and say, "I'm sorry for the things I said in the paper." And he would smile and say, "Hey, forget all that stuff." It didn't even bother him. When you really get right down to it, he's a pretty good guy. When I was having problems in my marriage to Jo Jo Starbuck, he and his wife, Marianne, offered to let me stay at their house. I couldn't face him today without feeling deeply grateful to him for those kinds of things.

I want to go back to Pittsburgh and walk out on the field at Three Rivers Stadium, stand next to Chuck, and tell him I'm there to support him. That may never happen, because Chuck isn't very easy to approach. But that's how I feel. We all grow up.

In 1988, when Chuck was enduring another losing season and going through some difficult and stressful times, I began to feel guilty about how much I was second-guessing him as a member of the media. The last thing he needed was me attacking him. He needed me to defend him; I feel as though I have let him down. I was one of the guys who started all the criticism of Chuck. And now I regret every negative thing I've ever said about my ex-coach and wish him nothing but the best. Even if I never get a chance to see him face to face, I hope he will accept this as my apology.

3

A HUCK FINN EXISTENCE

I come from a working-class family. My dad, William Marvin Bradshaw, lied about his age when he was eleven so he could drive a log truck. Told them he was seventeen. He grew up poor and grew up hard and had to leave the family at an early age. He met my mom, Novis Genoa Gay, when he was in the Navy, stationed in Pensacola, Florida. He met her through one of Mom's brothers, Carl. They dated about four times, got married, and have been together ever since.

Mom was from Hall Summit, Louisiana, which consists of Lawson's Grocery Store and Slim's Barber Shop. I think the town might have expanded to include a bakery. It was about 1958 before they got their first stop sign. They probably had an unveiling.

My family was poor, but that never stopped us from having good times together. My fondest childhood memories are of the farm in Hall Summit owned by my mother's parents, Mamaw and Papaw—Clifford and Estelle Gay. We used to go to Hall Summit on Friday nights when my dad got off work. My brother Gary and I—Craig wasn't born yet—would climb in the back of Dad's Chevrolet truck and off we'd go. It was absolutely the most thrilling moment of my childhood. Two of my cousins, Len and Greg, lived on the farm with Mamaw and Papaw, and the four of us would have a grand time.

I idolized Papaw; he had a heart bigger than Texas. Everybody loved him. Papaw just never said anything bad about anybody. He was a gentle, tender man, and my mother worshipped him. Papaw taught me a lot about hunting and fishing and farming, but he taught me a lot about life, too. He would tell me: "Never say 'never,' because 'never' is never a word. There is always going to be one time."

First thing I would do when we got to the farm was rip off all my clothes and run around in my underwear. My brother and I were in heaven. The four of us played hide-and-go-seek and stayed out late and roasted marshmallows. We'd take straight pins, bend them into hooks, cut down limbs, tie on some kite string, use a twig for a bobber, and catch bluegills. Sometimes, on a hot day, we'd go skinny-dipping in the pond.

Mamaw took care of the cows and taught us how to milk them. Papaw had chickens and a 'tater shed for sweet potatoes and a salt shed where he cured his bacon. He had a barn made out of logs; that's where he kept two Clydesdales, Tony and Shorty, that he used as his plow horses.

If we arrived on the farm while it was still daylight, we'd run down to the field if Papaw was plowing. He'd put us up on Tony and Shorty. I still remember the smell of the two big Clydesdales sweating in the hot Louisiana sun as Papaw walked behind that plow. That's where I first learned to love horses and I dreamed of someday owning a piece of land where I could farm and raise horses. I can still smell that freshly turned dirt and will never forget the feel of it between my toes as we ran through the plowed field.

My Mamaw continued to pick cotton when she was pregnant with her last child, Uncle Bobby. One day she left the field, went to the house, had the baby, cleaned it up, and went back out to pick more cotton. Tough stock.

In the morning, you could hear Mamaw beating on the

kitchen counter, kneading the dough for biscuits. She would choke them off, squeeze off "cat head" biscuits, and put them in the oven. While the biscuits were cooking, she'd fire up the coffee pot. I'd wake up in the morning and get a whiff of that coffee—the best aroma of any coffee I ever smelled. I can remember it as clear as a bell—chickens clucking in the back yard, roosters crowing at dawn, and a cool breeze sweeping across the porch. Mamaw would come out there with a fly swatter, and we'd act like we were still sleeping. One of those flies would land on us, and she'd pop us with that swatter.

To reach Papaw's two-holer outhouse, we had to run down a cold, wet trail, and our legs took a beating on the briars. At night we'd take a bath in a number-two wash tub. Mamaw would draw the water from the well and it was colder than ice—you talk about quick baths. You throw your bar of Ivory soap in there and jump in for thirty seconds. Great way to conserve water.

We boys were always getting into mischief. When Mamaw was milking the cow, we'd sneak up on top of the tin roof over the barn and drop the cat to see if it would land on its feet. Mamaw would be slapping the cow on the side to get more milk. When the cat landed on top of the cow, sometimes the cow would kick at Mamaw and knock the milk over and she'd give that cow a whack. We'd snicker so hard we'd almost fall off the roof.

On Sundays, you could hear Mamaw chasing chickens around in the back yard. When I heard a chicken squawk, I'd run to the back yard because I was always fascinated how the chickens would run around after their heads were chopped off. Boyhood curiosity. She'd fry that chicken and cook corn, peas, onions, green beans, and turnip greens from the garden. And, of course, she'd make biscuits or cornbread.

Going to town with Papaw was a big event. He'd load his cotton in the back of his wagon pulled by Tony and Shorty. All of us kids would jump on that truck and hold the cotton down on the three-mile ride to the cotton gin. Papaw would get his money, and then he'd go buy us an R.C. Cola and a Moon Pie. We wouldn't want him to take the top off our R.C. Cola. We made him take out his knife and cut a hole in the top so we could suck it out. That way the drink would last longer and you felt like you got more for your money.

Other times Papaw would take watermelons to town in his 1952 Chevrolet truck, maybe take them in to Elm Grove and peddle them along the oil fields, or maybe just sit at the crossroads and sell them.

It was a regular Huck Finn existence, one that I will always treasure. I hope my children can someday experience similar pleasures when we visit my ranch in Grand Cane.

My parents were loving, but they were stern. We were raised with a lot of discipline and had a very happy childhood. They didn't spare the rod, and I got my share of it. The worst whipping I ever got was for lying. I made the mistake of lying to my dad about a baseball glove that belonged to Mr. Robinson, my coach. I went over to a vacant lot to play ball, and I lost it on my way back. Mr. Robinson came to our house for his glove and I told him it was in the closet. It wasn't, of course, but I went back to the closet to act like I was looking for it. The whole time I was in there, I was thinking, "How in the world am I going to get out of this?" Next thing I knew, my dad was back there, and he was very unhappy. He beat the tar out of me.

Usually it was Mom who gave us the spankings. Like other moms, she'd try threatening us: "Wait until your dad gets home." And when Dad arrived, I'd come out and grab his lunch pail, get the newspaper for him, and say, "Hi Dad, how are you doing?" He'd very seldom spank us.

The worst part was having to go out and cut your own switch to get whipped with. The key was you had to find something that didn't hurt so bad. But if you brought back the wrong kind, a stick she didn't like, you'd get it even worse. She'd grab that switch in one hand and me in the other and off we'd go around in circles.

"No, mama, I won't do it no more."

"Come here."

"No mama, please, mama . . ."

I would kick and squirm and she'd whip my legs with that switch until they felt like they were on fire. Oh, did it hurt! It seemed like I got spanked constantly when I was growing up.

Gary and I shared a bed. And I used to get terribly embarrassed when I peed in the bed, which happened quite often when I was a kid. The next morning, I'd roll Gary over on my side and say, "Look, Gary, you peed in the bed." I don't think I fooled him.

The fact that we were poor never occurred to me because I never missed out on anything. I never lacked much, except for a few material things. And my idea of rich was anybody who had button-down shirts. If they had button-down collars like Dobie Gillis or Wally Cleaver, they were rich. If the wife wore a dress in the kitchen, they were rich. And if they drove a Thunderbird, they were millionaires. But I always dressed neatly in my J. C. Penney slacks and had clean underwear and clean socks.

I always shared my problems with my parents, even after I left home, because I respected their opinions. We are still very, very close. When I was playing football, I'm told my mom would watch on TV and would get so nervous that on a crucial play, she'd get up and walk out of the living room. If I got hurt, she would start crying. In 1970 when I hurt my hamstring, my mother came up to Pittsburgh to be with me. Her baby was getting operated on and she wanted to be there. When I came out of the operating room, still under anesthesia, I cried out, "Where's my mama, I want my mama!" I wasn't embarrassed in the least bit that she was there. I wanted my mother there. That's the kind of relationship we had. Her baby was a long way from home for the first time and she wanted to make sure I was okay.

When I got drafted and was signed by the Steelers, the first thing I did was fill my mother's house with furniture. I was dating a girl at the time whose parents owned a furniture store out in West Texas. I sent my mother out there and told her to buy whatever she wanted. I think she still has that furniture today.

If I could model myself after one person, it would be my dad. He is extremely motivated, very intelligent, and a self-taught man. He worked himself up through the ranks and recently retired as a vice president of a manufacturing firm. He was well liked by the men who worked for him. He motivated them. He made sound business decisions. And, most of all, he is morally strong.

For a long time Dad wouldn't tell us he loved us. He was raised differently and it wasn't manly in his day to admit out loud that you loved your sons. We'd say, "Dad, what if something happened to you, or to one of us. We might go to our graves never hearing you say you loved us." He finally got over the hump and now he tells us he loves us all the time. I've got very special parents. I hope I am respected as much by my kids.

Friendship is a very precious thing. When I was growing up, the one thing I always had was a close buddy. When I was a toddler, my best buddy was my brother Gary. We lived in Iowa and didn't have many friends, so we did everything together.

My first buddy outside the family was Tommy Spinks. It was tough to find receivers sometimes in the pros, but it was tougher to find somebody to play catch with when I was a kid. It wasn't until the Bradshaw family moved into a new Shreveport neighborhood that I finally found my main man Tommy. We immediately became best friends in the eighth grade. He lived close to me and we played catch every day. He loved it as much as I did.

If I had played another ten years in the NFL and added up all the passes I threw in games and practice to Frenchy Fuqua, Lynn Swann, John Stallworth, Benny Cunningham, Franco Harris, Jon Staggers, Jim Smith, and Ronnie Shanklin, they would never top the number of my passes that Tommy Spinks caught. He replaced all the rooftops, trees, swing sets, and bedroom ceilings in my life.

Tommy, in fact, was an excellent athlete. Phenomenal basketball player. Even better at baseball. And could throw

the football on the dead run. I'd go over to his house to play
catch on Saturdays, and we'd throw the football the entire
day. I had a stronger arm, but he was a better athlete. We'd
go up to the vacant field at Woodlawn and play our imagi-
nary championships, starting on the five-yard line. We'd
break out of the huddle and run our two-minute offense
against the clock. I'd announce the game as we played it: "It's
fourth down and twenty, ball at the midfield stripe. . . ."
Tommy would haul in my pass, step out of bounds, and get
almost as excited as if he were in a real game. Tommy could
catch anything.

But there was this problem: he, too, wanted to be a quarterback. Tommy played ahead of me most of the time on the
"B" team all through our sophomore and junior seasons. He
also started as a defensive back. So I developed my strategy
to convince Tommy he ought to play something beside quarterback. I would brag on him.

"Tommy, you've got great hands. Best I ever saw," I'd say.
"You ought to be playing wide receiver. Let me go talk to
Coach (Lee) Hedges about it." Sure, enough, I went to the
coach and said, "Tommy wants to play wide receiver, not
quarterback. We've been working out all summer and you
ought to see him catch the football. Great hands! He wants
to play wide receiver, but he's too shy to say anything." And
Coach said, "Well, we'll try him out there, if that's what he
wants to do." I went back to Spinks and said, "Okay, Tommy,
I've got it set up for you to play wide receiver." Tommy went
on to become my number-one receiver in high school and
college.

I was a conniving rascal, but I just had to have that quarterback job.

You talk about hot uniforms—the Woodlawn High
Knights had them. About twenty different color combinations of red, white, and blue. The local newspaper even did a
feature story on the tremendous number of combinations.
They said we could go through two entire football seasons
without wearing the same color combinations twice. Woodlawn was big-time high school football, competing at the

Triple-A level in Louisiana. And there was plenty of competition.

I didn't start on the varsity until I was a senior. We only had one returning starter my final year at Woodlawn and were picked nearly last in the district. Our offensive line averaged 150 pounds, and we were a running team. I outweighed most of my linemen by forty pounds. Tommy and I were determined not to let our senior year slip away. We literally lived football twenty-four hours a day, spent the night at each other's houses, and dreamed the dreams of teenage boys when their lives are filled with expectation.

Woodlawn had a good season my senior year and wound up going to the state finals before losing 12–9 to Sulphur High School in a rainstorm; I threw an interception that killed us. I had a fair season, completing about 47 percent of my passes, but didn't even make All-City. Our big star was Tommy, who caught more than fifty passes for a dozen touchdowns, and was voted All-City, All-District, and All-State. Had it not been for my showing against Lafayette in the state semifinals, when I threw two touchdown passes, I might not have gotten many football scholarship offers. I had plenty of track scholarship offers after setting a national high school javelin record (244', 11")—as many as two hundred inquiries from interested schools. But football was my sport and the only reason I had thrown the javelin was to keep myself in shape during the off-season. I didn't throw javelins in the trees and on the roof when I was a kid—I threw footballs. And I wanted to be a college football player. I often wonder what might have happened if we hadn't moved into the neighborhood where Tommy Spinks lived.

Tommy and I eventually grew apart, I'm sorry to say. He lives in Dallas now and has four kids. I went to see him recently; a few months later he played in my golf tournament, which raises money for the Make A Wish Foundation. I hope we can rekindle our friendship—it would mean a lot to me.

4
DEALING WITH THE "DUMB" IMAGE

When I arrived in New Orleans for Super Bowl IX against the Vikings, the onslaught began. "Terry's Brain Up for Scrutiny" said the headline in the *Post-Gazette* back in Pittsburgh. I wasn't sure if I was in town to play the G.E. College Bowl or the Super Bowl. I had just hit town to play the biggest football game of my life, and the reporters blitzed me with questions about my intelligence, which, for some reason, had become an issue.

"What's your I.Q.?" asked a writer. I was stunned and angered by his question, so I shot back: "I don't think that's any of your business. I don't want to talk about it because I'm tired of discussing the matter."

But that didn't stop him. "Is it true you really wanted to go to LSU instead of Louisiana Tech?"

"No, not true at all. I made up my mind to go there because I liked the people and the atmosphere."

"What did you major in there?" asked another reporter.

"I beg your pardon?"

"What kind of grades did you get?"

"That's none of your business."

And so it went.
The birth of a dummy.

I once attempted to trace the origin of the "dummy" label, but to no avail. But I'm tired of chasing ghosts and I finally gave up due to lack of interest. The best that I can tell you according to documented information I've received is that my own coach contributed to that "dummy" image. And maybe I'm partially to blame for the times I played the "good ol' boy" role.

The way to deflect a negative image is to make fun of it along with everyone else. After all, what was I going to do, start bringing books to the locker room? They were already convinced I was stupid based on the way I played in my early years. So the answer to overcoming that stigma was to play better and to poke fun at the image. It was not always easy.

Being called dumb hurts about as bad as any pain I ever experienced. It was grim walking into the visiting stadiums where the bench is close to the stands and have fans yelling at you: "Hey, dummy. You're so stupid you'll screw this up! Come on, Ozark Ike! You're so stupid, Bradshaw, you can't find your way back home!" I would cringe when I heard the word "dumb."

I'm not a combative person, but hearing somebody call me "dummy" was the only word that could make me so mad I wanted to fight somebody. But once you're labeled, you're labeled for life. Even though people might say, "Well, he was a good quarterback," or "He was a nice guy," they'll always add, "He overcame his dumb image."

Thank goodness my wife is young enough that she never knew anything about this "dummy" stuff, because you never live it down. She might not have ever married me; she's extremely intelligent and she certainly doesn't want to be "Charla Bradshaw, wife of 'Dummy' Terry Bradshaw." I pray to God twenty-five years from now when my children are grown that everybody who knew about me being called "dummy" will be dead and gone. Can you imagine your children going to school and hearing the kids ask: "How's that dummy daddy of yours?"

Being called dumb is the most deprecating term for a human to endure—not just a football player, but any human being. Can you imagine the embarrassment that it caused my friends and family? Multiply it times a hundred and that's how it felt to me.

There could be dozens of reasons why somebody thinks you're dumb, among them being a southerner. I'm proud of being from the South, of talking slow, and being raised by a southern mom and dad. I'm proud of everything my heritage and family have given me. Some people judge you by your accent, however, and folks in Pittsburgh might have been guilty of that at first.

Another possible reason for being labeled dumb is that I struggled in my early days. Understandably, people had doubts about me. The way I played on the field, I was hardly a candidate for NFL Rookie of the Year in my first season, as I've already admitted, but we really didn't have much of a team. I set a club record for interceptions as a rookie with twenty-three and only had seven touchdown passes. My critics in Pittsburgh were saying the Steelers wasted the number-one pick in the NFL, but the truth is we didn't have much of a supporting cast at first. And rookie quarterbacks always start out poorly—even John Elway did. Once, in his rookie year, Elway lined up behind a guard to take the snap. So it happens to us all.

As a rookie, I was totally lost. I was nervous and uncertain trying to call the plays, and I sometimes stumbled on my words in the huddle. The media comes to a player like, say, Rocky Bleier and asks him how I run my huddle. Rocky replies, "Well, he keeps changing the plays in the huddle. He says, 'full-right split 36—no, no—full-left split.'" Now the word is out that Bradshaw stutters in the huddle, that he is indecisive on his play-calling and, frankly, not too bright.

Lots of quarterbacks think out loud in the huddle, because while you're calling a play, another one pops into your mind. Even late in my career I still stuttered in the huddle because I was always changing plays right up to the end. That's normal. When I read Bleier's comments, they really hurt me. So I discovered the best plan of action was to be

firm, call a play, and act like it's the greatest play on the face
of the earth. And maybe your teammates would believe it,
too.

People assumed that because I stuttered, I was indecisive
and therefore dumb. When my own teammates would give
credence to the dumb image—sometimes innocently, I might
add, because Rocky didn't say it maliciously—things would
worsen. You just can't imagine how much they throw at you
as a rookie, especially when you're so green that you don't
even know what a zone defense looks like. I had the additional burden in 1970 of having beaten out a local hero,
Terry Hanratty, from nearby Butler, Pennsylvania.

I actually played pretty well at times, although we only
won five games that whole season. I threw for more than 200
yards in two games, but we lost in Denver and Cleveland
because our field goal kicker, Gene Mingo, missed makeable
field goals. After the Denver game, Chuck decided it was
time to start rotating quarterbacks. Hanratty would play a
half and I'd play a half. Any fool knows you can't do that
with quarterbacks. All rookie quarterbacks experience
trauma. And even in those losses, I was gaining confidence.
Had my coach been wise enough to understand that, he
would have stayed with me. We may have won more than
five games, but he had to act on it then and more or less pin
the blame on me. By benching me, all that did was add to my
dumb image and, of course, tear down what little confidence
I had. After I became successful, nobody talked about my
indecision in the huddle anymore, but that's just an example
of how one legend grows and one dies.

To make things worse, four years later Chuck brought in
Joe Gilliam, a black quarterback from Tennessee State, and I
lost my job to him. In my fifth season I was a failure. Racists
were making fun of me and saying I must really be dumb
because I'd been beaten out by a black quarterback. The
Gilliam thing was a mystery, but I've been told that Chuck
was getting heavy lobbying by Lionel Taylor, his black assistant, to make Joe the first regular black quarterback in the
NFL. It was not only embarrassing to lose my job to Joe—not

because he was black, but because he had beaten me out—but it was sickening the way Chuck fawned all over him. He would make me stand up and fine me in front of my team-mates, but he let Joe get away with anything—including sleeping during most of our film sessions.

Another source of the "dummy" tag may have stemmed from the story about taking the college entrance exams for LSU and eventually going to Louisiana Tech. Peer pressure is an amazing force. I was a great one for trying to please anybody and everybody. So when it came time for me to choose a college, I got wishy-washy. Unless you've lived in Louisiana, you can't believe the importance attached to such matters as what college a high school football player will attend. Naturally, Louisiana folk are partial to their biggest state university—LSU. One minute they had me convinced that I'd never be able to say I made it unless I competed against the big boys at LSU. The next minute, another group from Louisiana Tech was telling me I'd get lost in that big student body at Baton Rouge.

I really thought I wanted to go to Baylor. First time I ever got on an airplane was to make a visit to Waco. Don Trull, quarterback for Baylor, was one of my heroes—he and wide receiver Lawrence Elkins teamed up to become one of the most explosive passing tandems in the Southwest Confer-ence. Both of them played for John Bridgers, a coach I admired. But when I got to Waco, I was bitterly disap-pointed—not so much at the program or the coach, but at what I observed. I just wasn't mature enough for what I would see of campus life.

On my first airplane flight, I felt about as out of place in the plane as I would on the Baylor campus. It didn't take me long to figure that Baylor wasn't the place for me. Mostly it had to do with my sense of values, which was being tested. At one point in high school I had considered going into the ministry and, upon hearing about my plans for the pulpit, Baylor began to recruit me fairly seriously: I was a Southern Baptist and Baylor was a Baptist school. When I arrived on campus, I stayed in the dorm room with a former player from Byrd High School in Shreveport. It was quite a revelation to me to learn that he smoked and kept whisky underneath his bed. I couldn't believe it when he offered me a drink, which, of course, I declined. A football player doing this was bad enough, but a football player doing it at a Baptist college was unthinkable to me. Immediately I jumped to the naive conclusion that everybody at Baylor smoked and drank. It just didn't fit my picture of what college football players were supposed to be about and it certainly blew my image of potential ministerial students.

Nothing seemed right. It was totally unnerving when they offered to fix me up with a Baylor coed. I told them no because I didn't want to be unfaithful to my girlfriend back in Shreveport. At that stage in my romantic life, the most I had ever done with a girl was hold hands and kiss. But I was "going steady," and that meant you didn't cheat on your girl. Whatever it was I expected to find was not evident. So I declined the party invitation for recruits and sat alone in a dormitory room, thoroughly dejected, not comprehending any of this.

It probably would have been the same at most other college campuses, but after my experience at Baylor, I figured it wasn't all it was cracked up to be. And I couldn't get over this boy from my hometown being a smoker and drinker. So I flew home to Shreveport with another broken dream.

This discouraging experience was confusing and I became a prime candidate for another mistake. I was a home boy and didn't have any confidence in myself, didn't think I could play major-college football. I felt I had to attend a small school in order to play. If I went to a big school, they would bring in all those great All-Americans one year and they would beat me out. I was scared to death to leave home, scared to death of a big college. Yet, at the same time, I liked the challenge and if I was going to follow my dream, my chances of getting into the pros would be better if I went to a major college. So despite my insecurity, I began to lean toward LSU, one of the most successful college football programs in America.

Down there in Baton Rouge when they play "Hold That Tiger" at Tiger Stadium on a Saturday night, you can't see anything but purple and gold. It is truly one of the most exciting and colorful stadiums in America and I was duly impressed. The decision was already tough enough with just Louisiana Tech, LSU, and Baylor involved. But following the Louisiana State High School All-Star game, another couple of dozen colleges jumped on the bandwagon: Florida State, Alabama, Arkansas, Notre Dame, the academies, Texas A&M, TCU, Mississippi State, Mississippi, Tulane, and maybe a few dozen other small schools or junior colleges. I didn't know until years later that we had a few illegal offers, because my dad kept them from me. One school offered $25,000 cash, which was all the money in the world to my dad—because he didn't even make that much in a year. Dad, of course, turned them down without even telling me.

LSU turned up the heat and began to recruit me heavily. Charley McClendon's team had just come off a Cotton Bowl victory and was on a roll. The state of Louisiana was divided—at least in high school football talent—between north and south. The majority of the population was in the south, around New Orleans. Shreveport, Ruston, and Monroe were in the north. Normally, LSU didn't recruit many quarterbacks in the north, because the Tigers were looking mainly for the rollout types. North Louisiana high school coaches were advocates of the pro-style offenses with dropback passers.

Trey Prather of Shreveport, who had preceded me by a year at Woodlawn, was a great drop-back passer and the hottest thing to come out of Louisiana since Cajun gumbo. There was a lot of pressure on LSU to recruit Trey, so they went after him and he signed. LSU was running the sprint-out passing attack and, naturally, Prather wasn't fitting in very well. All that weighed on my mind. Billy Laird was the first of five star quarterbacks out of Woodlawn High School, followed by Prather, me, and John Booty and Joe Ferguson, who both went to Arkansas. Ferguson, of course, became a fixture with the Buffalo Bills during O. J. Simpson's heyday.

So the talent in north Louisiana was beginning to surface

and LSU, realizing this, made a push in our area. Some very persuasive LSU alums began to recruit me. Nobody from LSU offered anything illegal, but a local guy in Shreveport let me drive around in his Mustang for a few days. (Under today's absurd NCAA rules, that would get you ten years of hard labor.) Later, one of the LSU alums drove me to Baton Rouge and all the way there it was pressure, pressure, pressure to sign. All the way back: pressure, pressure, pressure. On the return trip I finally succumbed, stopping to call the people in Baton Rouge and tell them I would sign with LSU. They sent a guy to Shreveport and I signed, but I was miserable from the first day. My heart just wasn't in it.

Because of my decision to sign with LSU, I became very unpopular with some of the people closest to me. My coach, A. L. Williams, wouldn't speak to me anymore because he had wanted me to attend Tech. My girlfriend—the one I refused to cheat on while visiting Baylor—broke up with me because she said her brother was going to Tech and she had planned to go there, too, and now I had gone and messed up her plans. I was getting hit from all sides, thinking maybe this LSU business wasn't such a good idea. This set the stage for my reverse.

When I failed the LSU entrance exams the first time, that became my out for not attending there. They asked that I give the entrance exam another try. But the next time I took it, I doubt if I got one question right, because I didn't read them. Just went right down the list and made a Christmas tree. I wanted out of the LSU pressure cooker and into the security of the small school in Ruston, Louisiana, about ninety miles from Shreveport. Besides, my brother Gary and most of my friends were already at Tech. I didn't want to attend LSU, and flunking the ACT test seemed to be the easiest way at the time. I had no idea that I'd pay for it years later and that this would come back to haunt me. And if I told the truth about not trying to pass the entrance exam, it sounded like a lame excuse.

I found all kinds of reasons for not going to LSU, but the most legit was the lack of a pro-style passing attack. Prather, a sophomore, hadn't exactly set the woods on fire. Besides, he was a high school All-American and I started thinking, "I sat behind this guy two years at Woodlawn High School, so why would I go to LSU and do the same thing?" At Tech, coach Joe Aillet believed in the pro system. It all added up: I had to be a Louisiana Tech Bulldog. And guess what? I was able to pass the entrance exam without a hitch. Louisiana Tech turned out to be perfect for me: small school, personal attention, small crowds, small-time schedule. No media to speak of, no TV, and no interviews. It was just what I needed: a chance to play and mature. Except for one thing. The program was sort of in a shambles, the players weren't very good, and the attitude wasn't very healthy in the first two years.

The starting quarterback was Phil Robertson, whose passion was hunting and fishing, not football. All he wanted to do was fish, hunt ducks, squirrels, and deer, and roam the woods. He used to walk barefoot into the dressing room before a game with fish scales all over his clothes, maybe a squirrel's tail hanging out of his back pocket, and blood on his shirt. And he'd say, "Boys, them ducks was flyin' high today . . . we got a deer this morning . . . we got twenty-six squirrels . . . boy, them bass were poppin'."

I've got to be honest and say that I thought I should be starting over Robertson, but the worst was yet to come. I must have had a knack for making bad decisions, or so it seemed when Joe Aillet resigned as Tech's coach before my sophomore year. We had only won one game my freshman year and they told us he resigned—I don't know, maybe he was fired. Regardless, he was being replaced by Maxie Lambright, who was big on the running game.

Upon hearing the bad news, I contacted a friend who got in touch with people at Florida State who had said, unofficially, that they'd be happy to have me transfer to FSU. So over the summer between my freshman and sophomore years at Louisiana Tech, my brother Gary and I hopped in the car and drove to Tallahassee. When we got there, I stopped at a gas station, called my FSU contact and was told,

"Get out of here! We can't touch you. We don't want anything to do with you. You're going to get us on probation." Gary and I were devastated by the news; on the drive back home I was at an all-time low.

When I got back to Tech, I heard the good news: Robertson, my competition at quarterback, had quit the team. And coach Lambright had decided to stay with the pro offense, with me as quarterback—at least for the time being.

I was scheduled to start the first game my sophomore year, 1967. Maxie called me into his office and told me I had earned the job, that he didn't want Phil back, and that I would be in the lineup when we opened against Delta State. Finally! I was going to be a starter. What I didn't know was that Maxie, my coach, was canvassing the alumni, asking them what quarterback he should play. Phil Robertson was not only a good quarterback, but he often went fishing with some of the key alumni. Naturally, they were big Robertson backers.

So what happens? A few weeks before we played Delta State, the coaching staff went to Phil and begged him to come back (I found this out later). They didn't bother telling me, of course, and when we loaded the bus for Mississippi, Phil got on. It was great news to all the players—everybody but me. When the news hit that Phil would be starting ahead of me, I totally lost it. We were warming up on the field before the game when Maxie walked up and said, "I'm going to start Phil." I screamed, "What?!" and threw the ball as hard as I could right at him, as if I thought I could kill him with it.

Justice, however, prevailed. Phil got knocked unconscious on the first series of downs. I went in and threw for more than 250 yards and we won. The next week I started, but we lost to McNeese State, so Maxie started Phil. If Phil had a bad half, I'd play the second half, or vice-versa, and that's how it went my sophomore year. After a season of that garbage, Phil finally got tired of it and quit—this time for good. The job was mine as a junior. Louisiana Tech built a new stadium that seated 25,000. We beat teams like East Carolina, Mississippi State, and Southern Mississippi, won nine games and lost two, went to the Grantland Rice Bowl, and beat Akron. I threw for three touchdowns and ran for two to win the MVP trophy. My childhood pal and high school teammate Tommy Spinks caught twelve passes in the game and we set four records. I wound up leading the nation in total offensive yardage my junior season. So I guess Louisiana Tech turned out to be the right place for me.

To summarize my feelings about the "dummy" issue—and with the writing of this book, I plan to leave it for good—I am convinced that the media grabs a label early in an athlete's career and never lets that athlete live it down. An image is not always something that's based on fact. And if you don't do anything to disprove it, then the image grows. You come into the NFL with great expectations and fail to deliver, and critics start looking for reasons. If you're running for your life, dashing out of the pocket, doing things out of the norm, it becomes pretty obvious something is missing. In my case, I couldn't read defenses as a rookie and I didn't have much help. Twenty-six interceptions tells you that.

Some of the responsibility for the "dummy" label may stem from the Pittsburgh media. One guy in particular I've always wondered about was Sam Nover, a TV sportscaster from WPXI-TV. Sam was especially friendly with some of the players and always seemed to be up on the latest team gossip. He was a young hotshot from Detroit and was going to take the Pittsburgh market by storm. I used to sit in my locker and marvel at his social antics. He was always hanging around the guy who was hot—a real bandwagon jumper. Old Sam was like a rattlesnake: if you stepped on his tail, he would bite you, but if you didn't bother him, Sam was a good ol' boy. He was the kind of guy I never trusted. I'm not going to say Sam was the guilty party, but if those kinds of comments were being made in the locker room, then I've just got a feeling Sam knew about them.

Finally, the finger points right back at Chuck. The one documented case of my being labeled a "dummy" stems from him. It was a story I never knew until I heard it from Babe Parilli.

"It was Terry's second year," Babe said. "We were driving, moving right down the field. Chuck sends in a play. He calls a fake trap in the middle and a roll-off to the right. First down. We got four downs to make it in from the one. We call a split right, quick three thirty-three. Terry loses ten yards.

"Chuck shouts 'dummy' at Terry on the field, but Terry can't hear him. I heard him. So Terry runs it again. Loses another fifteen. Now we got third down and twenty-five. Chuck says, 'Run it again, dummy.' Terry runs it again, loses more yardage. We are on the fifty yard line by now and have to punt the ball. We lose the game by a field goal.

"There were some things like that which happened on the sidelines in those early years which Terry wasn't familiar with, but I was."

According to Babe, Chuck told him he was going to employ the "good cop, bad cop" routine with me. "He told me he was going to be the bad guy, and I was the good guy," said Babe. "He said, 'Now, I am going to chew his ass out and you take care of him.'"

I loved Babe. When he came in my second year, I immediately improved. He didn't stay around but a couple of seasons and now I understand the reason. Maybe now you can understand, too, why I was so confused about Chuck Noll. Considering our conflicts, perhaps it's a miracle we ever went to the Super Bowl, let alone won four of them.

5

CORNERSTONE OF A DYNASTY: MEAN JOE GREENE, FOOTBALL MACHINE

The Pittsburgh Steelers of the '70s were a rare collection of men. We had great pride, reveled in the "nasty" image, and never failed to remind our opponents that we were tough guys from Steeltown. Once we got a taste of the pie, we wanted it all. It's difficult to stay on top, as NFL teams discovered in the '80s. But the Steelers' hunger pangs were boundless and that's why we won four championships in six short years. Like the Los Angeles Lakers of the '80s, Green Bay Packers of the '60s and New York Giants of the '50s— teams that were able to keep generating championships back-to-back—the Steelers remained motivated throughout the mid and late '70s.

Pro teams in today's world seem to lose sight of their goals from one season to the next. As the years go by and I see teams trying to repeat, I almost chuckle to myself. The more Super Bowls I see, the more I say to myself: "Uh-huh, you boys are making all the money, doing all these commercials, getting all this fame, but when you try to do it again, it's not so easy, is it?" Then the modern players try to say, "Well, it's not as easy to repeat as it was back when you played." And I say, "Okay, that's cool. But it wasn't the same for us as it was for the Green Bay Packers, either." So you can't say that.

In my travels around the country, I sense it's beginning to dawn on pro football fans just how remarkable the Steelers' accomplishments really were. When they were reminded that we won four titles in six years, sometimes it completely blows them away. Only now, nearly a decade later, are people beginning to realize just how dominant we were.

One of the reasons for our dominance was Joe Greene, the cornerstone of the Pittsburgh dynasty.

When I look back on my first year at Pittsburgh, with all the many things that I had to learn and endure, the one person that comes to mind first and foremost is Joe Greene. I'll never forget the first time I laid eyes on Joe coming down the hill to practice: socks down around his ankles, huge thighs, big Afro, jersey hanging out, looking like he had been up all night. What a sight! He was called "Mean" Joe Greene because he earned the name. He took cheap shots at quarterbacks, driving them out of bounds and into the bench if he could. He was ferocious. He couldn't be blocked because he was so overpowering. Joe Greene was something that the NFL had never seen before—he redefined the position of defensive tackle.

Early on in his career, Joe Greene worked hard at being a bad actor on and off the field. As the first real star on Chuck Noll's team and the number-one draft choice the year before I arrived, Joe already had a niche for himself. And, in some respects, not a very good niche. The first time I saw Joe, he weighed more than three hundred pounds and couldn't even jog around the goal posts before we did our calisthenics. We were worlds apart. I had my shirt tucked in, looking prim and proper, saying "yes, sir" and "no, sir," and here comes Joe Greene, AFC Rookie of the Year. We were all running around the goal posts and Joe was barely making it, saying nothin' to nobody, because he is not just Joe Greene, he is "Mean" Joe Greene.

Joe wasn't wearing knee or thigh pads. When practice

started, he was so out of shape from not taking care of himself and smoking tons of cigarettes that he could hardly do anything physical. Then one day I found out why they called him "Mean" Joe Greene. He got angry because the cooler was out of Gatorade and the ball boys were slow in bringing in refills. So he took his foot and knocked down a huge door with welded trim, just to prove his point. Joe wanted him some Gatorade. And he got it. Plus a five-hundred-dollar fine for knocking the door down.

I was dazzled by the media, afraid to say the wrong thing, always trying to please them. Joe took a different view: he treated the media with complete disdain. He actually spat on Pat Livingston, veteran *Pittsburgh Press* columnist—spat right in his face—during one of the early NFL players' strikes.

This man was mean, nasty, vile, tough, dirty—all the things I wished I could be and wasn't. After all, I was Terry Bradshaw, All-American boy, trying to be perfect in every way. And he was Mean Joe Greene, who didn't give a damn if anybody liked him. I guess that's why Joe became one of my heroes and best friends right off.

"Mean" was a way of life for Joe, and the name fit. He had a terrible temper on the field. When an offensive lineman would hold him, Joe would warn him: "Don't do that again." And if the offensive lineman held him again, Joe had his own way of dealing with him. He punched Paul Howard of the Denver Broncos in the gut right on national TV and it was shown on instant replay. Howard doubled over with pain and had to leave the game. I figure Joe said something to Paul like, "Now, Howard, don't hold me again. I know we're in Denver and I don't want to have to punch you in the stomach and knock you out, so don't hold me again." Paul held Joe. Joe knocked him out.

During the regular season at Philadelphia, Joe took the helmet off an Eagle and started swinging it like he was Samson with the jawbone of an ass. He kicked the center's tail, then took on a few more and nearly wiped out half the Eagles team. The referees chased Joe around Franklin Field before they finally caught and ejected him. Joe came running back on the field, stole the football from the referee, ran into the end zone, and threw it into the stands. Later that year, Joe did the same thing in Cleveland. "Mean" Joe Greene. Get it?

When Joe became successful, he dropped the "Mean." He became this classy guy who was still a great football player but had a different public image. It seemed to change about the same time Joe did that Coca-Cola commercial with the kid, the one where he tossed his jersey to the boy as he was walking through the tunnel. (That commercial, incidentally, won a Clio Award as one of the year's best.) Deep down, he had always been a pussycat, but we didn't know that. Joe just wanted everybody to fear him, because fear was one of his tools. And his tool sure worked on me.

The tools worked on offensive linemen, too. Among the stories about Joe's intimidation was this one, written by Pete Axthelm in a 1981 issue of *Inside Sports*, about how he intimidated five-time Pro Bowl guard Joe DeLamielleure of the Buffalo Bills:

"The evening before Joe DeLamielleure was to confront Joe Greene for the first time, the Buffalo guard (later traded to Cleveland) dined with reserve center Willie Parker, a college teammate of Greene's. Parker related how Greene had once bludgeoned an All-American lineman, ripping the player's face mask off his helmet at one point. 'Joe turned white as a sheet and went up to his room,' Parker remembers. 'He was up until three in the morning throwing up.'

"A year later, in a well-known incident toward the end of a game, DeLamielleure learned about Greene. When Buffalo broke its huddle, Greene had his foot on the ball. He said, 'I'm going to teach you white boys how to play.' DeLamielleure turned to center Mike Montler: 'Is he talking to you or me?' 'Both of us, I think.'

"The next two plays, Greene kicked the hell out of both of them. He kicked Montler in the groin. He kicked DeLamielleure in the lip. It was third down and three and DeLamielleure told the quarterback, Joe Ferguson, 'Throw the ball out of bounds. Please!' "

You can see why I was glad to have Joe Greene on my side. But another reason why I will always love Joe Greene is that he came to my rescue when I was a rookie. I was scared to death and needed somebody to reassure me of my place on this Steeler team, because it was going to be a bumpy ride. Joe must have seen something in me, because he showed his faith by saying: "Hey, man, you're going to be all right. You are our leader, the man we are going to win it with. Don't worry about what all those stupid assholes say. You are going to take us all the way. You are going to lead us. I just want you to know that." Joe warned all the reporters to get off my back the first few years and for a while they did. He always defended me for some reason.

Joe was my best friend on the team, even though we hardly did much together off the field except play a little poker together during the week. I loved Joe Greene. There was no other player on that team that I felt quite the same way about, although I actually spent more time with other players. My buddies on the Steelers team were Calvin Sweeney and Jim Smith, whom I played golf with; John Stallworth; and Ray Mansfield. It's funny now looking back at it, but only Mansfield was white. For a kid coming to Pittsburgh from the deep South, that was quite a revelation.

The scariest person I met in Pittsburgh—contrary to what people may think—was not Ernie "Fats" Holmes or "Mean" Joe Greene. The scariest person was wide receiver Roy Jefferson, whom I met in my first few days on the team in 1970. Ernie, also known as "Arrowhead" because he shaved his head in an arrow, merely shot at helicopters and grabbed reporters by the collar. Jefferson petrified me because he hated whites. Or, at least, I thought he hated whites. At my first Steelers' practice, fellow rookie quarterback Bob Leahy found out about Jefferson's temper when he accidently threw a ball behind him in a warm-up drill. Jefferson turned to Leahy and growled: "Don't you ever throw a ball behind me again!" I said to myself, "Bradshaw, you're in trouble, because you've got to throw passes to this guy." I could see myself dropping back in a game, spotting Jefferson in the open and my arm locking up with fear. When a quarterback strings out his receiver by throwing behind him, he becomes vulnerable to a shot in the ribs or the head by a defensive back.

Sure enough, Jefferson got open against Miami in a preseason game. I threw to him three times and he dropped all three. In a matter of days, Jefferson was gone. Roy went on to the Redskins to have a great career. But it was best for us he leave because, among other things, Roy had a bad influence on our superstar, Joe Greene, the first player ever drafted by Chuck Noll in 1969. And Joe was already regarded as the baddest man east of the Mississippi River.

Whether Roy really did have that much impact on Joe or not, I'm not sure, but in the eyes of Steelers management he did. I have talked to Roy since then and we laugh about it now—him being a black militant and me a redneck from Louisiana. Roy has changed, much for the better, and hopefully so have I.

Pittsburgh. An integrated city where blacks and whites socialize, play together on sports teams, and work side by side in the marketplace. It was a fact that never occurred to me until I moved there in my rookie season. Sometimes you need to experience a little pain in order to grow. My own prejudice came as a surprise to me, although maybe it shouldn't have. Racism exists today at every level in the NFL: against black coaches, black quarterbacks, potential black owners, right down to the black fans who can't afford the big money for high-priced season tickets.

For the most part, even the players discriminate among themselves—cliques on a pro football team are almost exclusively black or white. One of the characteristics of the Steelers championship teams is that we were able to bridge that racial gap and had no real cliques. Sometimes it's a case of black players wanting to be among blacks, so it isn't always the whites doing the excluding. We may have broken down some of the obvious racial barriers in our society, but there are still so many subtle ones. And I wonder sometimes if we even notice anymore.

If I learned nothing else playing football, at least I can say my black brothers and sisters taught me about their race. They must have gotten a kick out of observing my learning experience, because this was the first time in my life that I ever played on a team with blacks or was around them socially.

I simply had never experienced black culture. When I hit Pittsburgh as a rookie quarterback, it must have been like Opie from Mayberry getting off the train the first time in the big city. It didn't take me long to figure out that I was prejudiced. The first black teammate I ever talked with was Jon Staggers, the wide receiver from Missouri. This was the early '70s, when black militancy and Afros were very much in vogue; I think old Jon had been lying in the weeds waiting for a honky like me to come along. I was always terribly impressed by any player who went to a major university—regardless of his skin color—so whatever Jon had to say was going to bowl me over. I can just imagine what Jon was thinking when I arrived: "Hey, we got this redneck coming in from Louisiana today. I don't know what he's going to be like, so let's go down to his room and hear what he's got to say." So he did. And he found this very shy, naive kid who had lived a sheltered life in Shreveport, a small-college player who traveled mostly by bus to all his college games, hadn't been anywhere or seen anything, had no clue about the big-time media or how to deal with it, and was completely awed by this black wide receiver who had gone to a major school on a football scholarship.

I immediately became Jon Staggers's project. In a matter of minutes, I was picking up his jive talk and feeling confident that by dinner I'd be shaking hands like a black person, locking thumbs, and hanging out on the street with all the brothers. I wanted everybody to accept me and if I could act cool like Jon Staggers, my new black friend, maybe they would. Being straightforward, I just admitted to Jon right off I didn't really know very much about "coloreds."

"Hold it right there!" Jon said, and I could tell I'd already done something wrong. "Hold it! We don't say 'coloreds.' We say 'black.' " So I learned my first lesson about blacks, and clearly there were going to be many more for me. I'm embarrassed about it now, but the truth is that I was learning about my prejudice, something that is ample in the rural South. Since we didn't use the word "nigger" in my house and never thought the Bradshaws were better than anybody else, it just never dawned on me that I might have even the remotest racist thoughts or feelings. I think Jon sensed my innocence and knew that there was nothing malicious about my racism. So, hoping I could be salvaged, he set about to tutor me on black culture. I thought I was the only person in the world north of the Mason-Dixon line who was prejudiced.

Years later I learned just how rampant racism is in sports. And I cringe today at the incidents involving Al Campanis of the Dodgers and Jimmy "the Greek" Snyder, my former fellow CBS-TV broadcaster. I can honestly say that the times I was around Jimmy at CBS, I never heard him make any racist comments, but clearly he made them in front of a camera in 1987 and action had to be taken by the network. Do I think Jimmy the Greek was a racist? No. Do I think he made racist comments? Yes. And he paid the price for it. All of us are a little guilty of such indiscretions, however; I shudder to think what I must have said or thought about blacks before my enlightenment the first year I went to play football in Pittsburgh.

Today when I am stopped on the street in New York, Chicago, Pittsburgh, or some other NFL city and asked for an autograph, the chances are pretty good that the man or woman will be black. Why? Because I was a member of one of the greatest football teams in history, a team that happened to be predominantly black. The Pittsburgh Steelers of the '70s were much like the Brooklyn Dodgers of the '50s in that they had many black role models for young people to follow. You could go down the list of Steeler stars and more than half of them were black: Joe Greene, Franco Harris, John Stallworth, Lynn Swann, Mel Blount, etc. Consequently, as a member of that team, I am probably more recognizable in more black communities than white ones.

Over the course of the years with the Steelers, a good many of my best friends were black. I know that's a cliché, but for me it was true. In the beginning, however, my lack of knowledge about black culture made me very uneasy. My black teammates knew I was struggling with my personal growth and development in this area and they would set me up. At team parties, the black guys would send their wives over to ask me to dance. I know Joe Greene was behind this. I can see him hiding behind a pole somewhere and saying: "Honey, go over there and make Bradshaw dance with you. Heh, heh, heh, heh." And I'll never forget the night a black woman kissed me on the lips for the first time. I turned completely scarlet. Didn't know how to deal with it in those days. What if somebody saw me? I am ashamed to admit some of these things, but, remember, in those days, I just had never been exposed to blacks or black families in a social setting.

As a child, the only black person I really knew was a maid who came to our house. I couldn't understand why blacks were treated like inferior people. I remember that they couldn't drink at the same water fountains that we did and couldn't go into the same stores or restaurants. I felt sorry for black people. Why could I walk into a store and buy candy, but a black child had to walk in the same store through a back door? Even I knew that wasn't right. When we took a trolley to downtown Shreveport, we sat up in the front and the blacks had to sit back in the rear. My first experience playing against a black would not have been until my junior year in college when we played New Mexico State. But when I arrived at Pittsburgh, I never even thought about having blacks as teammates. It was intriguing to me. But it was as simple as this: if you've never had a can of Coca-Cola before and you drink one, now you've had Coca-Cola. So what's the big deal?

Generally, whatever racism that exists in our society is simply caused by a lack of exposure. Racism will never really be wiped out until our children have had a chance to grow up together and share each other's cultures. Black and white babies play together without recognizing any differences. That's the only hope for the two races to be completely compatible. That's one reason I don't want my daughter, Rachel, or any future children of mine to attend private schools—most of them are racially segregated. I want my children to grow up with black friends so they won't fall into the trap of racism that I did.

White people don't realize how fortunate they are. That was made clear to me as a child when I rode with my mother down to Cedar Grove, Louisiana, a predominantly black community, and saw these "shotgun" houses where they lived and wondered, "Why do they have to live like this? Why are they pushed all the way out here? Why do we have most everything we need?" From a human standpoint, it just didn't seem right to me. How would you like to be dumped on all your life, or kicked around, or have jokes made about you?

No wonder I felt uncomfortable when I first went to Pittsburgh. It was like starting my life over again. My ignorance wasn't by design; it was because of the environment I grew up in, and I struggled to overcome my background. Today, I think I understand the plight of the black man better than a lot of white people do because Jon Staggers, Joe Greene, Calvin Sweeney, Jim Smith, and other black teammates were willing to invest time in me as a human being. As a result, I have genuinely warm feelings for them.

So as difficult as those first few years as a Pittsburgh Steeler were, it was still a tremendous education. What better lesson in life can there be for a person than learning how to get along with another race? Dealing with my prejudice and overcoming racism was probably my greatest triumph as a pro football player.

Joe Greene has a loving, sensitive spirit that I appreciated in a special way. When I needed support, Joe gave it to me. And I will never forget that. People often want to know: was Joe Greene really that good? He was the very foundation of the Steelers' success. You build teams with defense, and Joe Greene was the bedrock of the Steel Curtain.

6

THE SCARECROW, FRANCO, AND MY MAN MOON

Jack Lambert was not like any rookie the Steelers ever had. At training camp, the veterans tried to haze Jack, demanding he sing the Kent State fight song. It's a tradition in the NFL to make rookies sing their college fight songs. Lambert told them, "Kiss my ass, I'm not singing anything." Jack Lambert never sang. He set his tone right off the bat. Nobody intimidated Jack Lambert.

J. T. Thomas, a starting cornerback, once said of Lambert: "He's so mean he doesn't even like himself."

I never really knew Lambert or had any kind of relationship with him, and I suspect most of his other teammates never did either. Maybe it was his natural dislike of quarterbacks, who, as he once said, "ought to be wearing skirts." Jack didn't hang much with offensive players or many of the Steelers, period. Often he would ride around with the Pittsburgh cops; one night, I'm told, that nearly got him killed. Lambert got into a scrape in a bar with a guy who turned out to be a member of a "death squad" that killed for money, although Jack wasn't the one who started the ruckus. The guy hit Jack over the head with a beer mug, and his policeman friend had to pull his gun to quell the disturbance. Today, this guy is serving a life sentence for first-degree murder.

Lambert was an intelligent, intense, boisterous, fearless player who cursed those teammates who didn't give 110 percent on every down. Don't give Jack Lambert anything but your best—he wouldn't tolerate less. You might not like Jack Lambert, but you always knew where he stood. He'd criticize our offense and sometimes we would fight back. We might say to him, "Look, you scarecrow bitch"—his nickname was "scarecrow" because his hair was always sticking out—"you get over there and play defense and we'll take care of the offense." But you knew Lambert only had one motive: he wanted to win. He couldn't stand to sit back and watch a guy not give his all, so he would tell him about it. He was a born leader, much more forceful than anybody on our team. On the field, he was in a runaway gear, adrenaline pumping twice the normal rate, totally focused on winning. He didn't even know the fans were there. Along with Chicago's Dick Butkus, Lambert was the best middle linebacker I ever saw.

I always wanted to know Jack Lambert personally, wanted to be his friend, but you didn't pick Lambert as a friend—he picked you. For whatever reason, Lambert didn't choose to be my friend. He's the one Steeler I never understood and he remains a mystery to this day. So I observed him from afar, respected him, and admired him.

Lambert dared to tread where most men wouldn't. If he didn't like a player turning up his music too loud in the locker room, he'd jump in his face about it and scream, "Turn that bleeping music off!" Often Mel Blount was the target of Jack's tirades, and Mel didn't back off an inch. I sat across the room and watched, fearing we were going to have a riot on our hands any minute. But Lambert knew how far he could go and what he could get away with. He always stopped short of offending anyone, especially Mel, our All-Pro cornerback who didn't fear anybody, either. The two of them argued like they were going to fight at the next word, but both seemed to get a perverse pleasure from their open threats, like two warriors rattling sabers or two gunfighters from the Old West about to draw on each other. I think it psyched them up. As the years went on, they called each other all kind of names, but it was almost like they were playacting for the rest of us, because it never went beyond verbal warfare.

Whether on the field or in the locker room, Jack Lambert never let up. And he was the inspirational leader of our team.

But there were some soft edges to the hard-nosed guys, too. Andy Russell and Ray Mansfield were already there when I arrived. I will always owe them a debt of gratitude for their kindness and support. When I first came to Pittsburgh and didn't know a soul, I went out to speak at a Fellowship of Christian Athletes meeting and the two of them showed up. That meant a great deal to me. I don't know if either of them had ever been inside a church, but they came out to hear me because they wanted me to know they cared. It was the kind of support a rookie seldom gets from key veterans.

Russell, the brilliant outside linebacker who had an M.B.A. from Harvard, was the leader of the Steelers in the late '60s and early '70s. He played for a decade starting in 1966 and was so smart he would often argue with Chuck Noll and challenge some of the things they taught at his position. Chuck didn't like Andy because he was smarter and knew the defense better. Andy is now managing partner in one of the biggest stock brokerages in Pittsburgh and owner of a coal company in southwest Pennsylvania.

Mansfield was a crafty center, a reliable and solid guy with tremendous football sense, who made me feel comfortable when he was in the game. He could diagnose any play and knew all the blocking assignments in the offensive line. Mansfield also had the perfectly shaped posterior for a center. He would stand up tall and his wide fanny made it easy to take the snap.

Those were two of my favorites. They threw a party for me at Andy's house to welcome me as a rookie. And when I got to training camp, they introduced me to beer through a game called "Cardinal Puff," which got me drunk for the first time

in my life. Then they played a prank on me: I'd just bought a
brand new Corvette and when I sobered up, I couldn't find it.
They had hidden it from me. Russell and Mansfield were the
NFL old guard. They were famous for going "over the hill" in
training camp: sneaking out after curfew for a few beers. To
me they were legends. I'd marvel at their courage because I
wanted to go over the hill too but didn't have the guts. Chuck
always put me across the hall from him in training camp so
he could keep an eye on me. Besides, I was the All-American
boy and couldn't be caught indulging in such stuff.

Ernie "Fats" Holmes and L. C. Greenwood, who came
along later and joined the defense, were two players with
great heart. Ernie, who played college ball at Texas Southern, probably inspired as much fear in his own teammates
as he did in his opponents, because you knew "Arrowhead"
was capable of almost anything. You never knew what to
expect of Fats, because his reputation for allegedly shooting
at a police helicopter preceded him. What actually happened was that Ernie was driving to Pittsburgh on the
Pennsylvania Turnpike one night when he got involved in a
spat with several truck drivers, whom he apparently felt
were trying to run him off the road. Fats kept right on
driving through Pittsburgh, followed the truckers onto the
Ohio Turnpike, and pulled out a gun and started shooting at
them. Naturally, that soon attracted the attention of the
police. Ernie pulled off the turnpike and into a wooded area
and when police surrounded him, Ernie began firing at
them. He actually shot at a police helicopter overhead and
wounded a law enforcement officer in the leg. After that he
went into a psychiatric unit for a month, where, incidentally,
he was visited every day by Art Rooney. Today, Fats is out in
Hollywood, where he has landed several bit parts in movies
as a heavy.

Yet it was L. C. who was nicknamed "Hollywood" because
of his flair for clothes. He was one of the first players to
carry a man's handbag. Actually his old nickname of "Hollywood Bags" was the combination of two. Some of the players called him "Bag It" because of the way he wrapped up

ball carriers when he tackled them. L. C. also sprayed his shoes gold and wore them in every game, even though he got fined after each one because they didn't conform to league policy. After a while, the league just gave up and let him wear them. L. C., a defensive end from Arkansas A&M, definitely marched to a different drummer and wasn't always tuned into the beat of Chuck Noll. He should have been a Valentine writer—he was such a sweet guy. But when he rushed the passer, he'd tear the quarterback's head off.

On the other side was Dwight "Mad Dog" White, who was mean and nasty. The Browns always thought he was the dirtiest player in the league because Dwight would invariably get into shouting matches with Cleveland's linemen coming off the field on the runways. He was to the Steelers what Dexter Manley is to the Washington Redskins: a trench guy who loved taking offensive linemen apart. I loved Dwight because he was such a great con artist. He was a funny guy with a great sense of humor, but he stopped laughing on the football field. He came out of the hospital for Super Bowl IX after having a stomach virus and losing a lot of weight and played one hell of a game against the Vikings. Today, Dwight is the president of a predominantly black brokerage house in Pittsburgh.

The most confident member of our defense was Blount, 6'4" and 205 pounds; he would talk a great game in the papers and then back it up. He could run like a deer, jam, cover man-to-man, and take on the NFL's best receivers. He was an overpowering corner in the days of the bump and run; once he got his hands on you, he controlled you. He was to cornerback what Joe Greene was to defensive tackle. Somebody on the team gave him the nickname "Supe," short for Superman. When he retired, Mel opened The Mel Blount Youth Home for wayward kids and at the writing of this book owns a franchise for cellular phones in Pittsburgh.

Melvin feared nothing. He even threatened to sue his own coach, Chuck Noll, for his testimony in court that the NFL employed a certain "criminal element." Noll was actually testifying on his own behalf in court because he had made a statement that George Atkinson of the Raiders was part of a criminal element in the NFL. Atkinson sued him for that remark. But when Atkinson's attorney asked Noll if certain players on his own team weren't also considered the criminal element—Blount being one of those he named—Chuck admitted that they were. Then Mel turned around and started proceedings against Noll. I don't think it ever came to trial.

At the other linebacker opposite Russell was Jack Ham, who was a combination of intelligence, drive, and natural ability. He had great instincts and could react to the thrown ball about as well as any outside linebacker I ever saw, which is why he had so many interceptions. Jack was the best athlete among the linebackers. He was inducted into the Hall of Fame in 1988, a year after Greene was named. Lambert will be right behind them, and many more from the Steelers of the '70s will follow.

Whatever we lacked in ability on defense we made up for in desire—if there was one common characteristic of the Steel Curtain, it was tenacity. Those guys would get after you like the IRS. By Tuesday the defensive players were already hacked off in practice and the game wasn't for another five or six days. By Sunday, or Monday night, they were ready to kill.

Our offensive players had different personalities. Mostly, they were thinkers and they'd play mind games. Mike Webster was a verbal leader. Otherwise, most of them were just steady performers—Gerry "Moon" Mullins, Jon Kolb, Larry Brown, Sam Davis in the offensive line. And, of course, my two brilliant receivers, Lynn Swann and John Stallworth.

The star system among skill-position players can be very delicate but effective. Swann and Stallworth became embroiled in a very competitive battle to catch the football. At the same time, they still liked each other and never lost sight of team goals. I was extremely conscious of their little duels and made every effort not to side with either. If Lynn caught nine passes for 180 yards and John only caught two for forty yards, I felt bad.

In college I had three great receivers and I tried to distribute the football equally among them. At the end of the year, they had each caught about fifty passes. In the pros it's not quite like that. You read defenses more and go to certain players because of what the defense gives you. You can call plays that are designed for primary receivers. If there was a double flag route, with both players streaking down the sidelines and the coverage says "pick your side," I would naturally go to Swann's side, because he was the guy I felt most comfortable with in the early years. But that can cause problems in the star system. Catching the football for a living is extremely competitive—there is only one ball and five catchers in the lineup at once.

The receivers all had their own little ways of politicking with the quarterbacks, but mostly it was subtle. The only receiver who'd come over and ask why he wasn't getting more balls thrown his way was Stallworth. He'd say, "Am I doing something wrong? Is there a reason you're not throwing me the ball?" Jim Smith would walk over before a game and almost threaten me: "I want the damn football!" I liked that attitude; I knew he was going to bust his tail. But Swann was above asking for the ball, unless he could see in a game that he was beating his man. Then he'd come back in the huddle and mention it. Anytime a player like Lynn would bring me something in the huddle, I'd go right to him.

Swann, who came from Southern California, was a cute little guy with a bubbly personality whom everybody wanted to take home, like a Kewpie doll. Lynn was a great dresser, a great talker, and a smooth operator who attracted lots of ladies. And he could jump like he was bouncing on a trampoline. Lynn was brimming with confidence because he was a number-one draft choice who felt he was already big-time. John went to a small school in Alabama and was out to prove he could play big-time football. Swann said to himself: "I *am* the big-time."

I don't think the Steelers could have ever won four Super Bowls without superstars who were team-conscious, like Swann and Stallworth. They were both good team men, but they were extremely competitive with each other. Stallworth wanted the same respect that Swann had, but Lynn was the first pick in the 1974 draft and John was the fourth. And because Swann came in with more credentials, he broke into the starting lineup sooner. Therefore I was more familiar with Swann's style before I was Stallworth's. Lynn was flamboyant and the Steeler fans loved him. He was showtime. John was The Quiet Man who was every bit as good as Swann, and in some cases better. But each was different.

Stallworth was a picture of grace. His hands were just as good as Lynn's and probably a little softer. Both of them would catch the ball over the middle without fear of getting slammed by defensive backs. The difference was that when Stallworth caught the ball and got a step, you weren't going to catch him.

Swann was smaller and more combative verbally. He would take on anybody, including Jack Tatum and the boys from Oakland. Lynn wasn't that graceful a runner, but he was quick and ran good routes. He was excellent coming off the jam at the line of scrimmage and exceptionally courageous at going across the middle. He ran his routes fearlessly and he was a fighter. You shut him down one week and the next week he's going to come out with guns blazing.

Lynn was a tremendous leaper who could jump high and stay in the air for a long time, but Stallworth was about two inches taller at 6'2". Both Swann and Stallworth caught the ball in their body a lot, but if you had to say which one had the best hands, I'd have to say Stallworth. John was deceptively fast. People had the impression that Swann was the fastest receiver, but when Jim Smith, Swann, and Stallworth ran a footrace in training camp, they all ran 4.5 seconds in the forty-yard dash. And Calvin Sweeney, another wide receiver from Southern Cal, beat all of them. So Lynn and John were about equal in speed. And both of them were adept at setting up a defensive back. They'd lean in on one route and then go outside to catch the pass. After a couple of those, they'd come back to the huddle and say: "This time I'm going to lean in and go in." So now they had the defensive back off balance. They were very intelligent and great at reading coverages.

That's me—11 months old and very cute.

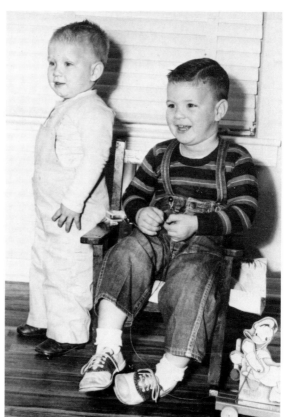

*Here's me (left) at 1½
with my brother
Gary, 2½.*

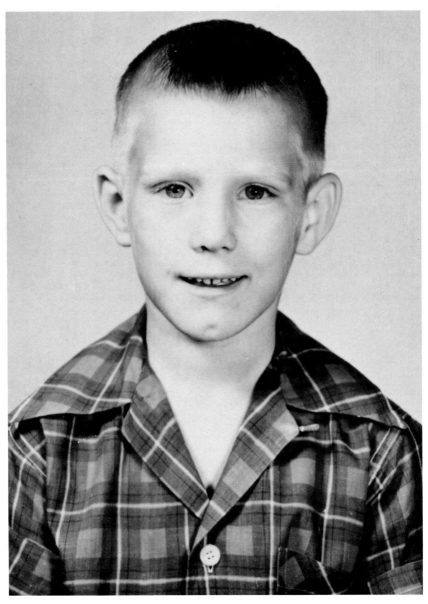

Here I am growing up; I was already throwing the football like a bullet.

Woodlawn High School's all-star quarterback ready for action.

*The Shreveport star—
posing for the local
paper was always
quite a thrill.*

The two faces of Louisiana Tech's quarterback—I've always been very serious about the game.

Can you guess what happened next? (Louisiana Tech, 1969)

Yes, that's me, hair and all!

Here I am at 24, sneaking out for a touchdown in a 1972 victory over the Raiders.

Throwing a few easy passes while recovering from a shoulder separation I suffered in 1973. Not to worry, though—I was back on the field in no time.

I think my expression pretty much says it all as I react to a play during Super Bowl IX (1975) against the Minnesota Vikings.

That's me calling the signals in Super Bowl IX, a 16–6 victory over the Vikings.

*Just catching up on the news before the start of Super
Bowl XIII against the Dallas Cowboys.*

This was a great day for me. The Steelers had a 35–31 victory over the Cowboys at Super Bowl XIII (1979).

Wide receiver John Stallworth sits on his helmet while taking a break during Super Bowl XIII. He caught two of my passes for touchdowns.

Here I am, dizzy from a concussion, taking it all in at the end of a long, hard day. These were the closing moments of Super Bowl XIII with the Dallas Cowboys in Miami.

Andy Russell (left) and I have a few laughs. That's my dad, Bill Bradshaw, in the baseball cap, smoking a cigar (1980).

Sporting my western attire as I relax before the start of Super Bowl XIV against the Los Angeles Rams in Pasadena, 1980.

That's me with Coach Chuck Noll right after my
touchdown pass in the second half of Super Bowl XIV.

"We're number 1!" The Steelers won an unprecedented
fourth Super Bowl victory, 31–19, over the Los Angeles
Rams in 1980.

On to the next phase of life—CBS Sports.

Here I am with my two favorite people: my beautiful wife, Charla, and my baby girl, Rachel.

Stallworth would come across the middle, too, and was outstanding at the deep route. He ran the sideline patterns better than Swann. Lynn appeared to be quicker and could get by the bump faster than John. Being taller, John was a bigger target for the defensive backs, but he was also stronger than Lynn. I think John was as effective as any receiver in the NFL at eluding tacklers once he caught the ball, and his ability to break free resulted in numerous touchdown passes for me that would have otherwise gone as long gainers. He has always said he was hungrier than Lynn and there were, indeed, times when his sheer will simply prevailed.

For ten good points about Swann, you had ten good points about Stallworth. I didn't have a preference. Stallworth was a secondary receiver most of the time because I was right-handed and it was easier to throw to Lynn. When Lynn became a perennial All-Pro, however, it seemed his dedication slipped. He began working for ABC-TV and had so many outside interests. I questioned whether football was really that important to him anymore. Some games he didn't get open when I thought he should have, so I began looking for Stallworth.

Meanwhile, John was hungry and he was coming on strong. I turned from a "right-handed" quarterback to a "left-handed," because I looked to John's side. At the end of Lynn's career, although I still had them both, John became my money receiver because I felt he was totally focused on catching the football. Lynn could still make great plays, but in my mind John was the guy who could get it done.

I liked Lynn a lot: he was in my wedding. In the last days of Lynn's career when the press was on him, there was a game during which I deliberately called everything for Swann. It was against Cincinnati in the early '80s and Lynn caught about 175 yards in passes for three touchdowns. And it got everybody off his back. I looked for Lynn every play without even reading the coverages. A quarterback can have that kind of control.

Quarterbacks and receivers have the biggest egos on most teams. I can hand off all day and even though I never do anything, at least I touch the ball. Receivers can't touch it unless somebody throws to them. And when it came to that, who better could I have had than Swann and Stallworth, along with my big, beautiful tight end, Benny Cunningham? In their time, Swann and Stallworth were the best tandem of receivers.

If there was ever a guy I wanted to make a star, it was Cunningham, a great big old sweetheart of a guy. I tried every way I could to get the ball to Benny, who was huge and could hurt people in the open field when he got loose. Benny would say in the huddle, "Brad! Brad! I can get open! Give me the ball, I can get by this guy." And I'd say, kiddingly, "Benny, you bitch, you haven't gotten by anybody all day!" It was a joy to play on the team with Benny Cunningham.

But I've saved this special place for a man who was without a doubt the most unselfish football player I've ever known—Franco Harris. From the very start, there seemed to be a cloud over Franco. He showed up late twice in a week for Penn State's practices prior to the Cotton Bowl game against Texas and Joe Paterno wasn't going to start him. I think that worried Chuck when he found out about it and he really wanted to use the pick on Robert Newhouse of Houston, but he drafted Franco number one in 1972 anyway and the Cowboys took Newhouse in the second round. Chuck's worst fears were confirmed when Franco didn't sign right away. One day in training camp at Latrobe, Pennsylvania, the phone rang in the scout's office and it turned out to be Franco's agent. Chuck got so mad he tore the phone out of the wall and threw it across the room.

When Franco showed up for training camp, he was very unimpressive because he never was a practice player. He certainly did nothing to get my attention in the first couple of preseason games against the Giants and Jets. That's not the way coaches like to see their number-ones perform. Frenchy Fuqua and Preston Pearson were starting ahead of him. Then, BANG! Against the Falcons in the third preseason game Franco exploded off tackle on a trap play and sprinted seventy-six yards for a touchdown. It became evident that he was here to stay.

Franco had a remarkable ability to read traps, find the daylight, bounce, pick, cut back, and fly. He wasn't a bruising runner for a fullback, even though he was 6'3" and 230 pounds. His forte was quickness and great vision of the field. He was more of a natural tailback with quick feet who could jitterbug outside and break it. Larry Csonka he was not. And some people criticized Franco for not taking the ball inside. I have seen Franco take licks and deliver them—he was capable, but he just never figured it was worth taking a direct hit for another yard when he already had the first down. When he stepped out of bounds a lot later in his career, it would drive some of the more macho fans crazy. If they knew Franco like I knew him, they wouldn't dare to question his guts or his manhood.

Franco was a man of few words and very little ego, but he was not above saying, "Brad, give me the ball" when he was on a roll. And that's the way most of the great backs were. I've never believed anybody when they tried to tell me a player was unselfish—all of them are selfish, including me. But I honestly think Franco was the most unselfish one I ever saw. He rooted for everybody and wasn't above becoming a guy's cheerleader.

We played the Packers in Milwaukee and it was a homecoming game for Bleier, who was a schoolboy star in Appleton and went to play for Notre Dame. I could have called Franco's number all day and we would have made twenty or thirty yards a pop on traps up the middle. Franco wanted Rocky to have the ball so he could block for him. And he would tell everybody, "Let's block for Rocky." He made Bleier look like Jimmy Brown that day. That's Franco, a true gentleman, a man for whom I have the greatest respect.

I know everybody wants to say their teammates were all wonderful, but Franco was a rare individual. Something very special. It hurts me that Franco was one of the superstars who never really got enough credit. One reason was that he never took advantage of being a celebrity. He was a master of the low key. He still lives in the same house in Pittsburgh. It's not right that he missed out on that one chance to break Jim Brown's rushing record as a Steeler because he and the Steelers couldn't come to terms on a final contract. Franco wanted to finish out his career in Pittsburgh, but my feeling is that Chuck didn't want him around and the ideal out was to have a contract dispute. He was picked up by Seattle and didn't last long out there. Franco retired in 1984 after playing only eight games for Seattle, just 192 yards short of Brown. Later, Walter Payton and Tony Dorsett passed them both, but that doesn't diminish Franco's greatness one bit. He was the featured back on four Super Bowl championship teams.

It's a shame the Steelers turned their backs on Franco, because it took away some of his heart and it was not a proper way to treat a true hero. Even if Franco would have only held Brown's rushing record for a season, or a few games, and then retired, it would have been a wonderful achievement. How sad. All Franco wanted to do was get the record for the city of Pittsburgh, for his teammates and himself, and then retire. Instead, he got the highway and never had a chance to say good-bye while still wearing Steeler black and gold.

One of the saddest things about Broadway is when they close down a play and the stars move on. The Steelers got long in the tooth. If you have an extended period of success, after a while you have difficulty getting motivated. And money becomes an issue if it hasn't already. Joe Greene suffered a shoulder injury and faded away. Ernie Holmes pretty much ate and drank himself out of football, so he was waived. Andy Russell retired. Jack Ham's career was shortened by an ankle injury. Mel Blount had a long career and stepped down. Jack Lambert was the victim of turf toe, one of football's most painful injuries. My elbow injury forced me out. John Stallworth and Donnie Shell stepped aside at the end of the '87 season.

The dynasty is over, and Chuck isn't going to be caught up

in sentiment. He's always prided himself on staying aloof from his players, even if they were on his championship teams. Ironically, it is that very success that has prevented the Steelers from getting those same high draft choices that came their way back in the '70s. The supply of talent couldn't be replenished fast enough. Chuck Noll has become a lonely hunter, pressing on, looking for the magic that will return the Steelers to supremacy. But what we had together as a team doesn't come in a wrapper or grow on trees. And if Chuck is the genius some people think he is, then he's going to have plenty of chances to prove that coaches, and not players, are responsible for dynasties. The jury is still out on that matter.

The relationship you establish with teammates lingers over the years, but it is more of a players' bond than a friendship. As much as I care for many of the guys I played with, I seldom talk to them. There are players on that team that I would like to see again. Mike Wagner, who played college ball at Western Illinois and was with the Steelers from 1971 to 1980, was one guy I enjoyed. He was just a good guy that I liked, even though I didn't hang with him that much. Mel Blount is a good person—a quality human being, like Joe Greene. I loved Dwight White because he was a character, a slick operator who made me laugh. Calvin Sweeney and Jim Smith were two of my all-time favorites. Ray Mansfield, Jim Clack, Gerry Mullins—all three were close to me.

Even though I didn't see that many of them socially, I felt good being around most of the players, except maybe Jack Lambert. We had a difference of opinion when I was working in TV and he was still playing, because it was my job to criticize the Steelers. Yet, I have great respect for Jack as a player and he is a good person.

Normally you pick out teammates and become buddies, so you run in pairs. Perhaps my best buddy was Mullins, who we called "Moon." He was a mover and shaker who knew all the bars, all the barkeeps, all the women. My friendships tend to be with people that I'm not like. Moon was from Southern Cal, a smart guy who played right guard and, despite his weight—only 230 pounds—was one of the few guys who could ever block Joe Greene. Later Moon would become my road manager when I was singing country music. We did some crazy things together. Moon was with me in Albuquerque when some crazed Cowboys fan pulled a gun on me. We had gone out to dinner when this guy stuck the gun in my ribs. I screamed, and several guys jumped the gunman and beat him up.

Of all the players, I guess maybe Moon was my main man. We hunted and fished together, and we double-dated a lot when we were both single. When you play pro football, you get a lot of mail and sometimes girls would send their pictures and ask you for blind dates. I could hardly wait to get my mail after I played well in a game. It was fun and it made us all laugh. If you got a picture of a nice-looking lady, you'd go around the locker room bragging to everyone.

So Moon got this picture of a pretty lady and began showing it off. She was a model from New York City, and she looked fabulous. She had written her phone number and Moon called her several times. Finally he decided he would ask her to fly to Pittsburgh for the Steelers' Halloween party. Moon went to the airport to pick her up and waited for what seemed like hours. Finally, she got off the plane and Moon was stunned when he saw her: this woman was ugly! She had sent a picture of somebody else. Right away, Moon wanted to ship her back to New York. But she cried and pitched a fit, so Moon took her to the team Halloween party, and the players gave him major grief. We laughed until our sides hurt. Moon had gotten stuck with a witch on Halloween.

The saddest day of my life, other than when I realized I couldn't play anymore, was when Chuck Noll cut Moon after he played nine years for us. If I could pick any ex-Steeler to live next door to me, it would be Moon. He's the one guy whose relationship I miss the most.

Making friends while you're playing in the NFL is not

always as easy as you might think. You learn as a rookie to be wary. People on the outside can't always be trusted. Teammates are here today, gone tomorrow, and if you invest in a relationship with one of them, you can suffer major depression after leaving the team abruptly. Athletes are always suspicious of anything that might affect their performance emotionally or otherwise. That's why the makeup of the football family is far more complicated than one might suspect.

7
THE FOOTBALL FAMILY

Much is made about the character of people football players associate with, especially since the incident involving Joe
Namath of the Jets back in the early '70s. Namath was
forced by Pete Rozelle to sell his interest in his Manhattan
nightclub, Bachelor's III, because of its alleged ties to
gamblers. Long before the Namath incident, however, Rozelle sent a warning to players about associations with gambling. In 1963, Rozelle made examples of Alex Karras of the
Detroit Lions and Paul Hornung of the Green Bay Packers:
both were suspended indefinitely for admitting to gambling
on NFL games. They had bet on their own teams to win. The
NFL Commissioner also fined five other unnamed Detroit
players two thousand dollars apiece for betting on games in
which they were not involved.

Since then, the league has clamped down on any players
even remotely connected to gamblers or gambling. The NFL
office sends a representative to every training camp to lecture players about associating with "undesirables," the
dangers of drugs, and other unmentionables.

No wonder pro football players are so paranoid. Athletes

on a team are like a big family and, naturally, you don't always like everybody in your family. But athletes believe that other athletes are the only ones that they can depend on and become very suspicious of outsiders. Players get closer and closer through the bond of the team; if you win, that bond gets even tighter. For this reason, athletes generally frequent the places where other athletes go—just like writers hang out with writers, nurses hang out with nurses, etc. That bond is sacred and the creed of the athlete is never to break it.

You may have a good friend outside the team and maybe you bring him along on occasion to a party or an outing, but he'll never be totally accepted by the players. Unless, of course, that guy can do you some good. If they are good guys and can in some way make your life easier or better, they are sometimes brought into the family. But athletes don't allow just anybody into the family: they've got to prove they are trustworthy and bring something to the party. And I suppose that's where some players become vulnerable to the "undesirable" element that the NFL warns you about. As soon as the outsiders do a small favor for you, there's an obligation on your part. I'm not insinuating anything illegal or immoral, but the danger is clearly there. Mostly, though, it's just small favors.

We had a guy in Pittsburgh who was accepted because he was a good friend of the Rooney family and took care of our traffic tickets. He was a well-connected Pittsburgh magistrate. Other guys provided us with spaghetti on Fridays. Guys we could get something from were welcome, because athletes are well known for having their hands out. But athletes are exploited in the same way, so it becomes kind of a tradeoff: you scratch my back, I'll scratch yours. Our traffic-ticket-fixing friend made money for some of the Steelers running the off-season basketball program, so we took care of him.

Most run-of-the-mill fans will never be accepted into the inner circle, however. Although athletes know the fans stroke our egos and we need them—especially to fill those seats—we also know that fans are as fickle as the wind. Rule Number One of most football players: never put stock in anything a fan tells you after a couple of good games, because all it takes is a couple of bad ones and he's on your tail. Rule Number Two: the only people who will ever love you are your immediate family.

When I played badly, the Pittsburgh fans hated my guts. Once they even cheered when I was injured and had to be helped off the field. There was a huge cultural gap between us at first: I couldn't translate what the fans were saying and they couldn't grasp my southern accent. They were used to hearing Terry Hanratty of nearby Butler, Pennsylvania, talk in their native tongue and it took a while for them to understand my Louisiana accent. After I began playing well and we won some Super Bowls, I was the toast of the town. You earn fans' respect by proving that you can perform. If you end your career with a team after establishing a worthy track record, they will embrace you forever. But before you get that track record, it's a hard road.

The truth is, athletes can never really level with fans or the press. If you're a member of a team and you live by its unwritten creed, you're not going to hang one of your teammates out to dry. After a game you can't say, "Did you see that the offensive line wasn't blocking?" or "Did you see those dropped balls?" because that will come back to haunt you. So you skirt around the edges of the truth and avoid the direct criticism. There were times when Swann or Stallworth or somebody dropped passes and I covered for them. There were times when I made poor throws and they alibied for me. It evens out. The minute you say something about a teammate, you are defending yourself and that's a no-no. So you take the heat. And those in the family know you are covering for them.

As much as I loved the fans, I could never totally trust them. The only people I ever really trusted were my relatives and certain members of my team. I respected fans and appreciated them, but there was no way I was going to be seduced by flattery and take them into my confidence as friends. Frankly, I doubt the fans really cared about being my friends anyway. Athletes tend to think their friendship is coveted by fans, but look at it this way: of the 250 million people in America, how many of them are Steelers' fans? A million? Maybe two million? Of those two million, how many of them do you think stayed up late that night after a game, worrying about how badly you played? Very few people out there are impressed with the Pittsburgh Steelers as a whole. And even fewer were impressed with me. I think we've blown ourselves up to be a lot bigger than we really are. Fans don't remember every play, every game of our career, and some couldn't care less.

When the Super Bowl was over last year, I didn't give much thought to who won, or who lost. I went home and went back to making a living, just like the rest of the fans did. The only ones who revel in the afterglow of the Super Bowl are people in the city of the winning team. Everybody else has forgotten. You'd be surprised how many people couldn't even tell you who won or lost the last Super Bowl.

I loved Pittsburgh fans. I was good to them and they showered me with affection. But I was never so stupid as to think that they liked me for any other reason than winning football games. Athletes are in the performing business and can't lose sight of that fact. Like most performers, athletes are generally suspicious, temperamental, high-strung, and insecure.

Players aren't nearly as suspicious, however, as league officials. Rozelle's biggest fear, of course, was that one day somebody in the NFL would be indicted for point-shaving or game-fixing and he'd wind up with a scandal like the 1919 Black Sox who threw the World Series. I've never known of an actual case where a player was involved in fixing a game. I have no doubt that gamblers ingratiate themselves with certain players just to gain information. But I have no first-hand knowledge of this—I'm only speculating. Point-shaving is not something that we ever discussed around the Steelers clubhouse, except when Rozelle sent his representative to lecture us.

Some coaches even put out a list of bars where they don't

want their players hanging out. Based on my experience, that's going a step too far, but I suppose it's an appropriate safeguard. When I was in a bar, other than the run-of-the-mill characters looking for inside information so they can win the office pool, or make an easy twenty bucks by betting on football with their neighbor, I never ran across anybody who appeared to be right out of *Guys and Dolls* or asked me to take a dive for them. But I'm not naive enough to think it couldn't happen or that I would immediately recognize a guy trying to fix a game.

A bigger problem in the '80s for the NFL has been drugs. For a long time it was as though the NFL denied there were any players who ever indulged in drugs. By 1988, with the NFL Substance Abuse Policy intact, the public was made aware of the problems through suspensions. Before the third game of the '88 season was played, nineteen players had already been suspended, including All-Pros Lawrence Taylor of the Giants and Dexter Manley of the Redskins. Then something worse: Atlanta Falcons special-teams player David Croudip became the second NFL player in three years to die of cocaine overdose when he drank a "cocaine cocktail" after the Falcons game against the Rams in October. Which leads me to believe we learned nothing from the mistakes of Len Bias, the rookie number-one pick of the Celtics, and defensive back Don Rogers of the Cleveland Browns, who died days apart in 1985. Apparently their deaths didn't serve as a deterrent.

At least the NFL Substance Abuse Policy, despite its flaws, is a step in the right direction. One wonders how a player like Croudip, identified since then as a regular cocaine user, could have escaped detection for so long. But at least the players are on notice that they can be caught and suspended. The first offense results in a thirty-day suspension. The second offense is worth a one-year suspension and the player is given another chance only if he goes into rehab. A third strike and you're out indefinitely. I applaud the NFL's efforts; if anything, they were long overdue.

Drugs were foreign to me in college. Maybe I was just

lucky to have attended a school where they didn't exist, but when I first went to the Steelers in the early '70s I had never even really heard of drugs until somebody offered me a stimulant in my rookie year, 1970. In the locker room before our game in Cleveland that year, a player showed me some pills. They were uppers, known as "greenies." I just looked at him and said, "I don't really need those."

´ Some players have the notion that the uppers get them fired up and make them play better. I had heard stories that in the old days trainers would pass around a jar of greenies, but I never had any conclusive evidence of that. You wonder why an athlete would need something artificial to make him play better. Football players always have sore bodies and I guess it's like running horses on butazolidin. The bute is bad, but it also enhances the horse's performance. It stops the bleeding in the horse's lungs making it easier for it to run up to its capabilities. I assume the greenies generate extra adrenaline and help numb some of the pain of nagging injuries for football players.

It's my understanding that Chuck Noll outlawed all uppers when he took over as coach of the Steelers. When I came into the league, some of the veterans told me that greenies had been around for a long time. Back in those days we didn't know that much about drugs and the National Football League was totally oblivious to any kind of abuse. In the late '60s, all the NFL worried about was a few characters making a few bets on games. Rozelle was more interested in suspending guys like Karras and Hornung for admitting they made nominal wagers on games.

Seems to me it was around the mid '70s when the drugs started popping up behind the scenes. Again, I wasn't considered to be one of the NFL's real party boys, and I wasn't playing for the Dallas Cowboys when Pete Gent wrote his infamous *North Dallas Forty*, a novel about drugs in pro football. So I can't cite you documentation, but I was aware of players smoking marijuana. And I did once see a Steeler sniffing cocaine. At parties, somebody would say, "Hey, we're going to step outside, c'mon with us" and I knew they weren't going out there to have a beer because the beer was inside. Grass was a pretty regular thing at most parties, although it was generally among a few players and the majority of them didn't participate—at least publicly. Marijuana seemed to be the socially acceptable drug—it wasn't like the evil heroin that killed Janis Joplin and Jimi Hendrix. I'm sure there were players around the league doing stronger drugs, but the only person I have first-hand knowledge about was Joe Gilliam, who later became a cocaine addict.

I actually saw Gilly doing cocaine before a Monday night game against the Los Angeles Rams at the Coliseum. It was the last game of the 1975 season. The Steelers had already clinched the division title and we were on our way to winning Super Bowl X. Chuck wanted to rest some of the regulars, so Joe started as quarterback. The lockers in the Coliseum are cubicles, so players are out of sight from their teammates. I just happened to stick my head over the top of Gilly's locker and saw him stuffing white powder up his nose with a little spoon. I didn't know what was going on, so I asked one of our linemen, Dave Revis, what Gilly was doing. Dave said to keep my eye on Joe. Gilly was wired. He was talking loud, jumping up and down, and acting like a wild man. Noll didn't know what was going on with Gilly. When the game started, Gilly would drop back to pass, start running, and when he'd get hit, he'd lie down on the field for a while. The trainers would help him off the field, then Gilly would go back in, get hit, stay down, and get helped off the field again. We lost the game to the Rams 10–3, breaking our streak of eleven straight victories, but it had no bearing on the playoffs.

The sight of Joe Gilliam putting cocaine up his nose only confirmed our suspicions. The signs were there. Today, those signs would be even more recognizable because they are more readily diagnosed. But this was 1975, and we weren't as sophisticated about drug abuse. There was no drug testing going on. We noticed that Joe was always sleeping during our film sessions. Terry Hanratty and I would laugh about it and we always wondered why Chuck didn't do anything. Gilly was constantly late for practice and each time he was tardy he'd have a new excuse. If it wasn't a sick relative, Gilly would fabricate a story about taking a cab and the driver not knowing how to find the stadium. One time Gilly said somebody had thrown a bucket of paint on his brand-new Mercedes and he'd been out trying to clean it off. Chuck even went out to the parking lot and examined Joe's car but found no traces of paint. Today it's assumed showing up late for practice and missing airplanes is a danger signal of drug abuse.

A person might ask why someone didn't go to Chuck and inform him that Gilly had a problem. After all, Gilly was a quarterback and at one time we had competed against each other, although by 1975 I had earned the starting job. I guess the reason is that you don't like to rat on your team- mates. If I had gone to anyone, it would have been Gilliam. I probably should have confronted Joe, but he would have denied it even had I gone to him. I guess that would have been a start, but today we know that people on drugs need more than just a friend to help. They need counseling, medi- cal assistance, and long-term rehabilitation. It turned out that Joe would need a lot of help—he finally snorted his way right out of the NFL.

The social dynamics of a football team are an interesting part of NFL life the public rarely sees. I'm told that on most teams there is a natural segregation among blacks and whites—not necessarily by design. That was somewhat true on the Steelers when I first joined the team, but it quickly changed. Blacks were usually on one side of the lunch room, whites on the other. I'll never forget one day back in 1971 when Mel Blount reminded Frenchy Fuqua that "you're a brother." Frenchy was sitting at an all-white table during dinner and Mel apparently felt he was making fun of the blacks. Mel isn't that militant anymore, but back then racial tensions were high.

As the blacks and whites developed trust and respect for

each other, soon the color lines weren't so evident on our team bus. Our team was not divided by race, either socially or on the field. It even got to the point where the blacks could make fun of the white players' expressions and vice-versa. You know you've crossed the boundaries when you can laugh at yourself, at each other, and with each other. During those years, many friendships developed between black and white Steelers. I can't recall any serious racial incidents. My closest friends—Greene, Smith, and Sweeney—were black. We said things to each other that people from the outside would be horrified to hear out of context. But it was acceptable among the family.

I imagine most racial barriers on pro teams have been crossed today. It was a little different back in the '70s, however, and the Steelers were one of the first predominantly black teams to be very successful. Back then when black and white players would go out to dinner together, we'd get some stares. I've seen it. I've felt those stares. Most of the time if I was eating with Smitty or Sweeney, people recognized we were athletes, but there was still a peculiar stare, different from the stares I got when I was out with a group of white teammates.

In terms of the cliques in the team itself, the players tend to follow normal social patterns: offensive linemen hang out with other offensive linemen; defensive players tend to prefer other defensive players as friends; and wide receivers are sometimes buddies, although the competition for pass receptions sometimes precludes that. The exchange between quarterbacks is the most interesting because they are so intensely competitive. The male ego and pride often get in the way of quarterbacks' befriending each other. A veteran quarterback may hang out with a rookie quarterback, because the rookie is no threat. But once the threat is established, then the relationship is severed.

Cliff Stoudt came up in 1977, after I was firmly entrenched, and I found him to be a fun guy. We played a lot of golf, laughed together, and hung out at times. But once he became a starter when I was hurt and down, our relationship got cold. He was trying to take over my job when I was coming back from an injury; I knew he wanted it badly. Suddenly there was friction between us, even though I tried to ease the tension by saying it was "Cliff's team" and not my team.

I will say this about Cliff: he was a real person, not a phony. You tend to accept a challenge from a real man. But a guy who presents himself through the media to the fans as somebody he's not—in other words, a hypocrite—is the one you can't stand. And once you figure him out, you can slice him up pretty good. He's history. At times I felt sorry for Stoudt because he never did get a real break. Although I still wanted my job, I didn't have any problems with Cliff, who had paid his dues. The other players liked Cliff, too, but unfortunately once he got a chance to win the job and the fans got on his back, he didn't handle that situation well. He spouted off to the press and taunted the fans. And it backfired on him.

Eventually, Stoudt left Pittsburgh and jumped to the United States Football League. Then the Steelers picked Mark Malone of Arizona State in the first round of the 1980 draft, but he never panned out. I initially liked Malone but later realized he was a phony. People said he looked like Tom Selleck, so he grew a mustache like Selleck, combed his hair like Selleck, and even wore flowered shirts like Selleck. He was always saying the right things to the press. After eight years of that stuff, Chuck finally traded Mark to San Diego. He was just too hip, and the players didn't appreciate him always pointing the finger at somebody else. Players won't tolerate a phony, which Chuck finally figured out. Malone was limited in ability and was probably better suited to be a wide receiver (that's what he played occasionally when he first came up) than a quarterback. Oddly enough, I threw the longest pass in Steelers' history—a ninety-one yard bomb—to Malone on November 11, 1981.

The most-liked player I ever hung around with on the Steelers was Terry Hanratty, with whom I shared the starting quarterback's job for a while. Everybody loved Terry, a consensus All-American at Notre Dame in 1968 and the number-two pick by the Steelers behind Joe Greene in 1969. Terry not only drank and caroused with the boys, but if we lost and the heat came down on the field, he took it rather than point the finger. He had a wonderful attitude about football. If he played a bad game, he said to himself, "So what?"

I was totally different. When I had a bad game, I was ready to jump off a building. I was not that well liked by other Steelers and could never have been as popular as Terry among my teammates. Everything I did was geared toward trying to accomplish some goal on the field. My main objective was to be as good as I could be and I didn't give a damn about social relationships on the team. I was there to do a job and when the job was over, I wanted to go home, not hang around with a bunch of football players. You are around players so much that you begin to lose your perspective on what the real world is all about. You're just fooling yourself, because that's not where your future lies.

Football is a great game, but it's only a stepping stone to a better life. It is a means to an end, not the be-all or end-all. It's not your life's work. Athletes and actors are living in a fantasyland—you're only as good as your last game or your last movie.

8

FOUR RINGS FOR THE BOYS AT THREE RIVERS

I used to lie awake nights when I first went to the Steelers, wondering what it would be like to play in The Big Game. At first I dreamed about getting to the playoffs. Then when we got to the playoffs, I began dreaming about getting into the AFC Championship Game, winning that, and going to the Super Bowl. It seemed our fans weren't satisfied with just making the playoffs. I guess it's true that when you set your goals high, you have to attain them to achieve satisfaction. Unless you hit the jackpot, everything else in between doesn't mean much.

Reputations are made in The Big Game. Every quarterback who makes the playoffs but falls short of making the Super Bowl is branded as a loser, a guy who couldn't get the job done, even though he may have played well and didn't deserve the rap. Big-Game quarterbacks are usually born, not made—there is no on-the-job training.

There are at least two quarterbacks playing today who I feel are better than I was: Joe Montana of the Forty-Niners and Dan Marino of the Dolphins.

When you start talking about great quarterbacks, the conversation usually begins with the one who is hot today. As we wrap up this book in 1989, Joe Montana is on everybody's mind because he took the Forty-Niners on a ninety-two yard drive in the last two minutes of Super Bowl XXIII to beat the Cincinnati Bengals. The Super Bowl win in Miami served as the coronation of Joe Montana, even if he didn't get named MVP.

But even without his performance in Miami, Montana would be right there near the top of most people's lists. His ability to run the two-minute offense and throw short touch passes were two qualities I wish I'd had. Some people will make a case for Montana being the best who ever played in the NFL, because he's got such a great lifetime completion percentage and he's won so many championships.

As Boomer Esiason said before Super Bowl XXIII, the bottom line for quarterbacks is winning championships. That's how you get into the Hall of Fame. Otherwise, why have championships? Why have high school district and regional playoffs, quarters, semis, and finals if it's not all about winning the title? So that forty years later when you're sitting around with a cigar and a cane, petting your dog, you can say, "Well, yeah, back in '65 we got to the state finals the first time in the school's history and lost to Sulphur"?

The memories are all about winning The Big Game—not statistics, or anything else. That's why Montana will go down right there with the greats. There is a certain quality about Montana, I think, that every quarterback has to have before he can be called great: he must be a leader, a winner, who has proven himself in clutch situations. If you really want to know how good a player is, go way back to his junior high days and see how he performed under pressure. Even if that young quarterback didn't win but one game, he may have found redeeming grace in one Big Game if he brought his team back against their archrival for a victory in overtime. How many big games did he pull out in high school? How about college?

Montana is a thoroughbred. His lineage has always been that of a winner, as far back as his days at Ringgold High in Monongahela, Pennsylvania. I remember reading about him when I was playing for the Steelers. What he did at Notre Dame was legendary, pulling game after game out of the fire. He was victimized by hypothermia when he brought the Irish back from a 34–12 deficit to beat Houston 35–34 with no time left on the clock in the 1979 Cotton Bowl. He had back surgery in '87 and many people wrote him off, but he overcame injuries to his knee, elbow, and ribs to prevail in Super Bowl XXIII. Frankly, I thought he should have been the MVP over Jerry Rice, but I guess they didn't want him to win it for the third time. Nobody ever has.

I love Joe Montana, and although our styles were entirely different—he throws short, I threw long; I called my own plays, Bill Walsh called his—he is a lock for the Hall of Fame. Maybe he will win another Super Bowl, which would give him four rings. Considering Walsh's retirement and the pending changes, however, that's not likely. And after all, Joe turned thirty-three prior to the 1989 season.

It's funny—when I did one of the Forty-Niners' games early in '88, I was talking to Joe about his situation, and he was very worried about losing his job to Steve Young. A few weeks later he was going to Disneyworld. That's quarterbacks for you—they're all basically insecure people.

There is a natural adversarial relationship between most veteran quarterbacks and their coaches. In most cases, the quarterback is out there busting his tail on the field and the coach is on the sideline calling the plays without the full appreciation for the problem at hand. Despite my trials with Chuck, he at least let me call my own plays most of the time. I don't think I could have ever played for him if he hadn't, although there were occasions when I'd beg off. I'd go to him after bad games and say, "Bail me out here, you call the plays for a while because the press is on my back." I did that about five times in my career and it usually lasted about one week. But even when I asked for help, I hated having Chuck call the plays. It was demeaning. That's like having somebody tie your shoes for you.

To really be in charge, you've got to call your own plays. In my opinion, any quarterback who calls his plays automatically has it all over one who doesn't. It's up to the quarterback in charge to distribute the football to the right players and make certain everybody gets a piece of the action. And when something is not going right, the quarterback who calls his own plays doesn't have to look over to the bench and hope the coach senses it.

Calling my plays gave me a better feel for the tempo of the game. If Franco's hot, I call his number. If Swann's hot, I go right back to him. If I need to go deep to Stallworth, I do it. All instinctively. You can't be instinctive when you're waiting for the play to come in from the bench. I don't say that to separate myself from the crowd, or to in any way denigrate other quarterbacks. But it's an important distinction, much like the difference between a songwriter singing his own music and somebody else's. When you are the composer, you know the proper phrasing. I suppose it helps the music when the singer's voice is good, but there's a certain accountability for both parts of your game, mental and physical, when you make most of the decisions on the field. And your teammates in the huddle tend to believe in you more.

So much of playing quarterback is confidence, and when I got to Pittsburgh, I lost all of mine. I had to start all over again and rebuild it, yet I never was able to throw the football the same way I threw in college. I believe in my heart that I could throw the ball a full 30 percent better at Louisiana Tech than I ever did in Pittsburgh—tighter spirals, stronger delivery, snapped the ball better. Even in my first Super Bowl I didn't have all my confidence because I'd been benched the whole year. But I will say that I learned more about developing a touch in the pros.

When your confidence level is up, you can take on the world. There were times with the Steelers when I actually felt I could control the entire outcome of the game. It's not conceit or bragging—it's a genuine feeling. When I was in my element and on a roll, I yearned for the moment when the game would come to one play. I loved it when I had to be The Man and everybody was looking at me to do something. You don't feel pressure. You feel relief in a way. It's almost like a sexual experience.

Other players get in that situation and say, "I gotta do it." Whereas some people know they *are* going to do it, others almost dread the responsibility. To me, the challenge was inspirational.

One never knows if he or she has that ability to perform under pressure until the chance comes, and the chance doesn't always come early for everybody. For me, it didn't come until my junior year in college, although we got close to it in high school and lost to Sulphur in the state finals. The turning point of my career came in our homecoming game against McNeese State. I had finally won the starting job and we were down a couple of touchdowns at the half. I know exactly what my stats were after two quarters: I was 4 for 16 with three interceptions. We had already upset Mississippi State that year and beaten a favored East Carolina team. During halftime I said to myself: "Boy, you're making a fool out of yourself. You're going to let this thing get away from you and destroy your whole career. You can't play like this!"

In the second half, I threw three touchdown passes and even had one called back. I can't tell you my stats for those last two periods, but I played well and we nearly won the game. That told me right there I had the ability to pull myself together under pressure.

Later on that year we were playing our big rival, Northwestern, in the Louisiana State Fair game. With twelve seconds left to play, I threw an eighty-two-yard touchdown pass to Ken Loberto and we won. That was my first experience as a hero, and I liked it a bunch. My confidence level was growing.

That put me in a good frame of mind going into my senior year at Tech. That's when I learned that through my God-given ability I could actually influence the outcome of a game by myself. I don't mean that I was a one-man team, but it was a hypnotic feeling that took over, and I felt as though I was in some sort of Twilight Zone. My confidence was supreme, and it was a very soothing, yet humbling, feeling.

When it happens, you can walk up to the line of scrimmage in a pressure-packed situation, surrounded by screaming and yelling, and yet feel calm inside. The tougher the situation, the calmer I got, the more in control I felt, and the more I could see. Later, in my second year with the Steelers, I was hypnotized by our strength coach, Lou Reckey. He gave me three key words—relax, confidence, concentrate—and each time I felt myself losing any of those, I just mentioned the word and it would come back. There was nothing mystical about the hypnotism, and I wouldn't recommend it to everybody, but it allowed me to focus better. And when you focus, you control your emotions.

In a big game you can't afford to get too high, because if you start feeling like Hercules out there, you force the ball into tight spots and make foolish mistakes. Mistakes take away your confidence. And when you lose your confidence, your antennae go up and you hear absolutely everything. You retain it all and everything bad has a compounding negative effect on you. When an athlete is truly focusing, he or she doesn't hear those things, and they have no effect. Nothing bad will happen to you to cause you to make a mistake. You will do the right thing because you are in control of all your senses. You're not affected by anything bad, or even good, that happens on the field.

Once you have control, you can throw an interception, the opposition can return it for a touchdown, and it doesn't have any carryover effect. I threw an interception against Houston in our second playoff game on our way to Super Bowl XIV, and the Oilers returned it for a touchdown to take the lead. I walked off the field totally unaffected, but I could hear some of my teammates grousing. On the sideline I said, "The guy made a nice play, they did a good job of confusing me, but it won't happen again."

I didn't panic or get upset. I was in control. We came back and won.

All the great two-minute quarterbacks—Johnny Unitas, Bart Starr, Ken Stabler, Roger Staubach—were confident that they could deliver when it counted. And they usually did.

My real love affair was with the old American Football League. I grew up with a great respect for George Blanda when he was in Houston, Lenny Dawson when he was in Kansas City, John Hadl of San Diego, Daryl Lamonica of Oakland—all those mad bombers from that "other" league. The AFL represented fun, which is what I always thought football should be, and the players seemed to enjoy themselves more than the guys in the NFL.

I absolutely loved Hadl and until Namath came along, he was my idol. I remember Greg Cook coming along in Cincinnati and thought he had great potential (Bill Walsh says he might have been the best quarterback prospect he ever coached until he was injured). I was very impressed by Bob Griese's intelligence.

Pittsburgh was in the old NFL back in those days and I never saw the Steelers on TV. Then they were rarely seen nationally because they were seldom any good. Since I was always watching the AFL on TV, I didn't see them the few times when they were televised. In Shreveport, when we got a doubleheader, the second half was always the Cowboys. I liked the Cowboys okay but never cared much for the NFL overall and found it boring for the most part. But I did like Roman Gabriel of the Rams and John Brodie because they both threw the ball a lot. But the NFL was mostly a running league and so the AFL was far more interesting to me.

I loved Namath for his style, because he had a way about him that was admired by everybody from the ladies to the media. I remember when I went over to introduce myself to Broadway Joe. He had a cop on each side of him, and the girls were screaming, and I said, "Now *there's* my idea of a quarterback." I rarely got to play against Joe because it seemed that every time we had a game with the Jets he was hurt. The one game he did play against us he did poorly. When the fans booed him, he gave them the finger. Joe could handle fans. He was cool.

When all the MVPs of the Super Bowl were introduced in New Orleans prior to the Bears-Patriots game in '87, Namath got the loudest ovation. He merited that because he was a star personality and a star football player, and the combination of the two made him bigger than life. Joe Willie Namath had it all: personality, charm, flamboyance.

I admired different qualities in different quarterbacks. Bob Griese had poise and he always looked in control. He could carry a team by himself, the way Dan Marino has had to carry the Dolphins in recent years. I think Marino is incredibly talented, even though he has never won a Super Bowl. He has a quicker release than I did and can read defenses better.

Kenny Anderson was a quarterback of great precision with the Bengals and he flourished in the system much the same way as Montana has done. Staubach was another one who benefited from the system, although he had that quality as a winner and a strong arm as well. Roger was a tremendous competitor—as long as he was in the game, I always feared that he was going to bring the Cowboys back.

If I had to pick one quarterback for one game, it would probably be Kenny Stabler. Rather than getting caught in the trick bag of rating quarterbacks, which I absolutely refuse to do (how could you ever discount the greatness of an Otto Graham, Bob Waterfield, or Sammy Baugh?), I'll simply say that when it comes down to the money players, I'll take Snake.

Snake was fearless. He looked deep and turned people around. Every pass was a perfect spiral. Could take a team downfield and "slide out." The epitome of grace under pressure. Would hold the ball to the very end before releasing it and take the hit. Remarkably accurate. When we played the Raiders I would get mesmerized just watching Kenny Stabler. I was jealous of him—he could do things I knew I couldn't do. And he did them gracefully. Our defense would get in his face and he still piled up the yardage, still threw down the middle, still threw outside. Kenny is absolutely my favorite of all time.

I've always liked the home-run hitter, the Big-Game quarterback who comes to life when the money's on the table. There is a myth that great quarterbacks play great all the time. Not true. Big-Game quarterbacks might play pretty well only during the regular season, but when the playoffs and The Big Game come along, they revel in it, almost as if they were born for that moment. They relish the spotlight and hardly ever play poorly when it's on them.

You can't really put your finger on it, because for the most part it's genetic: either they have it or they don't. Just because you lose in The Big Game does not mean you're not a Big-Game quarterback. Roger Staubach lost some Super Bowls, but he never played poorly. He didn't crumble under the pressure—the other team was just better. Sometimes that happens. Roger is certainly one of the best Big-Game quarterbacks the NFL has ever seen.

Fear drove me to avoid becoming a loser. I realized early in my career that I would never break Unitas's record for touchdown passes, I'd never break Fran Tarkenton's record for yardage. I'd never make it to the Hall of Fame on stats because of the conservative offense that we ran in Pittsburgh. And the only way I was going to set myself apart from the great ones was to become a Big-Game quarterback. Everybody wants to win championships, of course, but my whole career was targeted toward that goal.

About the only way I was going to gain respect from my peers was by winning Super Bowls, but I certainly got off to a rocky start. My first six seasons in the league won't exactly go down as banner years.

For a four-time championship quarterback, my statistics are somewhat embarrassing—212 touchdown passes, 210 interceptions, and only a 52 percent completion rate. But I do still hold a couple of Super Bowl passing records, like most touchdown passes.

In twelve and a half seasons over my fourteen years, I threw 3,901 passes, for an average of twenty-three a game. That's pocket change by today's standards. In just his first five seasons Dan Marino, all-time number-one rated quarterback by NFL standards, had already thrown 2,494 passes for 168 touchdowns. In 1988 he led the league with 4,434 yards and easily eclipsed a career milestone of 20,000 total yards. Marino has already thrown for 23,856 yards, averaging nearly 4,000 yards passing in six seasons. But he also threw the ball an average of nearly thirty-six times a game in a high-tech offense, compared to my twenty-three.

Of course the Dolphins failed to beat the Forty-Niners in Super Bowl XIX because they didn't have a balanced offense—they couldn't run the ball—and their defense couldn't stop Joe Montana. I don't kid myself—I'd never match Marino's stats, even in Miami's system. It seems, though, that a balanced offense and strong defense is the key to winning titles.

So I guess that's the only thing that I have: four championships. I'm very proud of that—the Super Bowl ring was the one goal I needed to meet in order to consider myself a successful quarterback.

I was fortunate to end up in Pittsburgh, but the Steelers weren't even in my top twenty-seven choices of the teams I wanted to play for. When I was a rookie, I made a statement that I was "happy to be here in Pittsburgh, because I want to be the first quarterback to lead the Steelers to the Super Bowl." I didn't really mean that and I certainly didn't feel it. But later on I got to thinking, "You know, if this team went 1–13 before I got here and one of these days we win the Super Bowl and I'm the quarterback, that will be a huge accomplishment."

You bet I was lucky to be in Pittsburgh. You bet I was lucky to have Franco Harris and Rocky Bleier behind me. You bet I was lucky to have Lynn Swann and John Stallworth on the flanks and Benny Cunningham at tight end. And Mike Webster and Moon Mullins and Sam Davis and

Jon Kolb and Larry Brown in the offensive line.

And a great defense anchored by Mean Joe Greene. That was probably our biggest asset, because it's so true that defense wins championships. I believe that more than ever now, because in three of the four Super Bowls—all but our last one—we were blessed with the Steel Curtain at its best. In Super Bowl XIV, we had to rely on offense. I'm not going to pretend I was the main ingredient in the four championships, especially in Super Bowls IX and X. But I'm very proud to have been a part of all of them, no matter how large or small my role. When everything else is moth-eaten, dog-earred and forgotten, those rings will still remain. I've always believed that you should try to be the best at whatever you do. When you're selling for a living, shouldn't you aspire to be the top salesman? Are you the president and CEO of your company? Are you listed in the Fortune 500? Are you the best garbage collector in your company? Is there a pinnacle for you in your business and, if so, are you there? Like it or not, you're going to be judged by how successful you are. And success in the NFL is winning the Super Bowl.

I think Al Davis says it best: "Just win, baby." The heck with the statistics—just win.

People today still marvel at the Steelers' consistency during that six-year period, especially in light of the so-called Super Bowl jinx that has hit teams in the '80s. Only two teams in NFL history through 1988 have repeated as Super Bowl champions: the Green Bay Packers in 1967 and '68 and the Steelers twice, in 1975 and '76 and in 1979 and '80. That makes me proud.

I don't necessarily think the Steelers were the greatest team of all time. You could certainly make a case for Vince Lombardi's Packers. Had the Super Bowl been in existence six years earlier, Vince Lombardi might have won it six times in eight years. I doubt if we'll see a team win back-to-back Super Bowls again soon, and I question whether any team will ever win four titles in six years. Parity has killed off dynasties in pro football and the great teams may have gone the way of the dinosaur.

When people asked me how the Steelers were able to win

so many championships, one motivation I point to is the importance of playoff and Super Bowl money to our players back then. The winner's share of the Super Bowl today is no big deal to the players, but back in the '70s, that money was a big incentive to the Steelers. Sometimes it amounted to more than half the salary of some players, because the Steelers were not exactly the highest-paid team in the NFL. Even though the winner's share in Super Bowls IX and X was only $15,000 and in XIII and XIV it was $18,000, that was big money to us. Postseason money became a means for our players to earn additional income—for adding on a family room, buying a second car, paying for the kids' braces and college educations. This is not to say other players on other teams weren't hungry—they just weren't as hungry as we were.

Since Super Bowl XVII, for instance, the winner's share has been $36,000, and that's peanuts to the guys making half a million and up. Nobody in football was making half a million in our first couple of Super Bowls.

The second reason, I think, we were so successful in Super Bowls is that we created a Steeler Mystique, which intimidated our opponents. Opposing players have told me that when they saw those black-and-gold uniforms on the field, it struck fear in their hearts.

The Steelers of that era were very talented, with the mental capacity, physical ability, and burning desire to be the best. The Raiders probably had as much potential talent as we did, but when it comes to the mental edge for one big game, no one could compare to the Steelers.

Finally, thanks to Chuck and his coaching staff, we were always prepared. Our offensive and defensive philosophies were fairly basic, and we knew that we weren't going to vary much for anybody in any kind of game. That worked for us back then, although it has proven to be a curse for Chuck Noll in the '80s.

As I watched films and reviewed newspaper clippings in researching this book, one thing that occurred to me is that championship teams must also have one very important element: luck. There's no doubt that we had a number of breaks that led to our four Super Bowl championships. All of those elements—luck, intimidation, motivation, simplicity, domination—are key in the development of a great football team. But none of those were as key as the element I think was most responsible for our success: talent. When they write the epitaph of the Steelers, I don't care what they say about how great we were, but they can never say we weren't talented.

9

FOOTPRINTS ON THE GLORY ROAD

SUPER BOWL IX
Tulane Stadium, New Orleans, Louisiana
January 12, 1975
Steelers 16, Vikings 6

There was nothing fun about the Super Bowl games themselves, but we made the most out of the week leading up to them. What comes to mind first about Super Bowl IX, down in my home state of Louisiana, is that the Steelers players went partying in the French Quarter right away. We ate oysters, drank a little beer, and talked a little among ourselves about the game, but mostly we relaxed, because we had already done almost all of our preparation. That's what Chuck told us to do—go down there, have a great time, enjoy ourselves, and play the kind of football we knew we could play.

It scared us that we had to play against Fran Tarkenton, one of the most prolific yard producers in NFL history. And it nearly psyched me. In practice, I wasn't throwing the ball well at all and began to worry. Hey, I was awed. I even went and had my picture taken with Tarkenton. Remember, this was Fran Tarkenton, according to statistics the greatest quarterback who ever played the game. He was the NFC Pro Bowl quarterback that year—a huge star—and I was a nobody. The only difference was that I was the home boy and he was playing on my turf. I was the star down there. So I went over and had my picture taken with him and marveled at his accomplishments, hoping he would respect me. Like any other quarterback, I wanted to be accepted by my peers.

If you've never been to the Super Bowl as a player, you really can't fathom it. The media is incredible—about fifteen writers or broadcasters per player back then and about three times that many now. But you don't get the flavor of the Super Bowl talking to the press. You get the real impact of the Super Bowl on game day when you go to the stadium and hear the people screaming and hollering. Drums are beating. Jets are flying overhead. Half of the crowd is hollering for the Vikings, the other half for the Steelers, unlike a regular home game where most everybody is rooting for one team. The Super Bowl stands are packed three hours before kickoff. When you walk through the crowd on the way to the locker room with a cop escorting you, people are hurling insults at you. There are fights breaking out between Steelers and Vikings fans. You walk in and sit down at your locker, and it hits you: "Holy smoke! This is unbelievable! This is what I've dreamed about. This is what I've worked my tail off for all these years. This is the Ultimate Big Game." All those breaks, all those bounces of the ball, all those ups and downs, all that hard work and desire finally culminated in one day: the Super Bowl.

As I sat there in the locker room reflecting on the moment, I suddenly began to hyperventilate. I couldn't breathe. My palms were sweaty. I went to the bathroom with diarrhea and I was so afraid of dehydration that I began drinking Gatorade. Then I began pacing up and down in the locker room. I must have chewed four or five packs of gum. I would look at my game plan sheet and couldn't see it. I was too nervous to focus on it. My brain was cloudy. "We can't afford to lose. This is the biggest game of my life," I said to myself. I couldn't stand the anxiety, so I sat down and lit up a cigar. I played cards. Other players around the locker room were so relaxed that they slept. My chest began to tighten up. And all I could think was: "We can't lose this game, it's too important."

I'd been answering "dumb" questions all week long. But now it was payback time. I could shut up every person who ever said anything bad about me. I could lead this team to a Super Bowl victory over the Vikings. And they weren't expecting me to do it. They didn't believe I was capable, because they thought I was too stupid.

I went out on the field to warm up, saw the fans, and was engulfed in emotion. Everywhere I moved, there was a camera in my face. There were more than a thousand members of the media in the press boxes and another couple of hundred on the sidelines. As I stood there, it dawned on me: "Every move I make today is going to be a part of history. Every call I make will be documented on film or in print. This will be on film in the Football Hall of Fame, because this is Super Bowl IX. Everything I do today will be part of the greatest thing I have ever done in my life."

Then an incredible thing happened as we returned to the field to be introduced. We were standing in line, waiting for our names to be called, when a Minnesota Vikings fan standing behind the ropes passed out and fell at my feet. He was lying there turning purple and, I guess, having a heart attack, because they were beating on his chest. The paramedics arrived and took him away; I never found out if he lived or died. As I sat there and watched them work on him, it made me sick to my stomach.

On the sidelines during the national anthem, the same emotions kept popping out: "Terry, play well today. Terry, be cool today. Don't panic. Don't worry about the pass rush. Concentrate on the coverages. Make the proper reads for audibles. Don't let the pressure get to you. You can do it, Terry. You're the best. And you can beat these guys. Just relax, take your time, and concentrate."

It's true, just like they say, that after the first play you're into the game, and all those emotions are behind you. Once it started I had forgotten about the famed "Purple People Eaters" or that Buddy Ryan was the Vikings' defensive line coach.

Our defense wasn't as heralded as the Vikings defense, but we shut down Tarkenton nearly all day. In the second quarter with no score, Fran pitched back to Dave Osborn and the ball got away from him. Osborn recovered in the end zone and Jack Lambert was the first one there, so he was credited with a safety.

It was a futile day for Fran, who kept trying to make something happen to no avail. We were up 9–0 in the third quarter and Minnesota had a fourth and one at its own thirty-seven yard line, so Fran tried to draw our defense offsides with a long count. Instead, both teams were ruled offsides and the Vikings had to punt. Every time Fran threw a pass, we either clobbered him or clobbered his receivers. Our defense totally destroyed him. In fact, had the Vikings not blocked Bobby Walden's punt—Terry Brown recovered it for the touchdown—they wouldn't have scored at all.

We were ahead only 9–6 with a little over ten minutes left in the game. Now it was up to the offense to keep the ball and put points on the board. I called Franco's number twice; he picked up eight yards on the second try, but we were still two yards short of the first down.

All of a sudden, I felt a sense of total control of this game. As I stood there around the fifty yard line, looking over the Vikings secondary, with the fans screaming, a sudden calm came over me. I felt invincible. It was like a flash of light: I knew what I was doing. I knew we were going to win this game. I'm going to drive them down. We *are* going to win! Nobody's going to beat us. I won't allow anyone to beat us. Our guys won't be denied. We got in the huddle, and I called a play and said with authority, "Now let's go! We need this! Break!" Boom! We were up to the line of scrimmage.

My teammates are looking at me and they feel what I'm feeling. They sense that I am in control, and it relaxes them. You can tell when they break the huddle and slap their hands together. We are moving as one, in body and spirit. The greatest feeling in the world is when you know you're going to win a big football game. During the day when it's hot, and you're standing out there on the field under the sun, for some reason it's not the same. But at night, it's like it's the only thing happening of consequence anywhere on earth.

You look up in the lights and you know the whole stadium is in your hands.

On third down I hit Larry Brown for thirty yards and a first down at the Minnesota twenty-eight. We get a five-yard penalty for illegal motion, and I call two more running plays, both to Bleier. The second one is an audible, and Rocky breaks it for seventeen yards down to the Minnesota sixteen.

As we move down the field, my teammates can see my confidence surge and they begin to feel it in the huddle. Now I can feel the pride swelling up in my body, like somebody is blowing air up my nose. I look at the sideline and every eye is on me. All the cameras are staring right at me. I can see the shock in the Vikings' faces. Now they are beginning to question whether they can get the ball back for Tarkenton. We've driving, they've got to stop us. And I know—I am absolutely certain—that they can't stop us. Because we are the Pittsburgh Steelers and we are going to win Super Bowl IX. What a feeling of joy!

A short pass to Rocky over the middle, two more running plays to eat up some clock, and now we're at the Minnesota four. Time out. Over to the sideline. "What do you want to run?" I ask Chuck. "Goal line three thirty-three," he says. A pass-run option outside.

I run back on the field. The fans are going crazy; there's nothing like being down at one end of the field, near the end zone, where you can hear the fans screaming. And if you score, you've won the game. And you know without a doubt you're going to put it in the end zone. I roll right, escape some pressure, push one guy away and see that Larry Brown has his man beat by an inch in the end zone. I gun it in there and he catches it for the touchdown pass. Gerela converts and we've iced the game with a little more than three min-utes left to play. The end zone is pure mayhem.

All of my life I had felt powerless, but now I finally was experiencing that feeling of supremacy, that feeling of su-preme confidence that Joe Namath talked about: looking out over that field and seeing the picture so clearly. It had been five years since I'd felt that confident about myself. It was like an old friend coming back to join me in a crucial situation.

I didn't set the world on fire passing (9 for 14 for 96 yards and one touchdown), but I called an excellent game, even if I do say so myself. Fran's numbers weren't much better: 11 for 26 for 102 yards. But he also had three interceptions and no touchdowns.

When the game was over and I walked off the field, I was not only physically drained but mentally exhausted. It was like the hardest work I'd ever done in my life. But a feeling of peace came over me and made me feel like saying: "Hey, I belong out here. They can never take this moment away from me." It's a feeling of quiet satisfaction. I'd done my job and I wanted to rest. I didn't want to party. I didn't want to go to a rooftop and shout. It was almost like I became depressed—I was coming down off that Super Bowl high.

I knew we'd won and done something great, but because I was so tired it really hadn't hit me yet. You feel you've answered your critics; the sad part about it was I really couldn't enjoy it because of my critics.

That week in New Orleans had been pure hell for me. I couldn't enjoy it, even in my home state, because I really hadn't been the Steelers' full-time quarterback that season. It had been up and down all year between me and Joe Gilliam. So I didn't feel I could celebrate with my teammates because I hadn't completely earned it. Gilliam had started the first eight games that year, and I took over the team on a Monday night in New Orleans and rushed for 99 yards. I felt I had only been a piece of the puzzle, and not a very important one, so I felt a little embarrassed to take any credit. After reading the papers I didn't have to worry, because I didn't get any credit anyway. The press only saw me as a small cog, if even that.

One of the nine passes I completed, the fourth-quarter touchdown to Brown, was the beginning of a little personal streak: a TD pass in the fourth quarter of every Super Bowl I played in. It wasn't until years later, when we began the research for this book, that I actually discovered this accomplishment, and I am extremely proud of it.

The most memorable aspect of Super Bowl IX was that Art Rooney, the grand old man of the Steelers, finally had a championship after all those years. I loved Mr. Rooney and felt a deep sense of satisfaction for him.

Franco had a tremendous game: he ran for a Super Bowl record of 158 yards in 34 carries and was named Most Valuable Player.

That night after the game, I went back to the room with my parents. My brother went out and bought a case of Cold Duck. We sat there drinking while my mother rubbed my head because I had a terrible migraine headache. Finally, I lay down and fell asleep while they played cards.

It was no fun for me, even when it was over. There never was a feeling of reaching utopia, like there would be in Super Bowls to come. I flew back to Pittsburgh, packed my stuff, and went back to Grand Cane, Louisiana, where I stayed for the entire off-season.

Now we had to repeat.

SUPER BOWL X
Orange Bowl, Miami, Florida
January 18, 1976
Steelers 21, Cowboys 17

Since I wasn't in demand for personal appearances in the off-season after Super Bowl IX, I spent most of my time at the Louisiana ranch, away from football. I worked out regularly and stayed in good shape, but I wasn't around a bunch of people who were telling me how great I was. So when I reported to camp that next summer, I had no feeling of superiority about anything. I knew it was going to take hard work to improve and to repeat as champions.

My six years' experience kicked in and I was starting to mature, but I couldn't be comfortable because I wasn't even sure I was the starting quarterback. I had to go back to camp and win the job. Our quarterback situation was up in the air because Chuck hadn't committed to either me or Gilliam.

I was hungry for the money, the attention, and the starting

job. But I also found out what it was like to be defending champions, because everybody seemed to play great against us. I'd see the teams on film, didn't figure them to be any great shakes, and show up on Sunday only to struggle right down to the wire. Chuck had warned us that everybody would play against us like it was their own Super Bowl, and he was right. Each week I had to get up for another big game and when the season was over, I was drained. There were no breathers. It was my first taste of teams saying, "We've got to stop Bradshaw." Ever so slowly, the Steelers had begun to depend more and more on me as a passer. Finally, I found some consistency and wasn't getting benched anymore. This might have been the most critical season of my career, because I finally began to grow up. The Steelers were 12–2 in 1975, won the AFC Central, beat the Baltimore Colts in the first round of the playoffs, and defeated the Raiders 16–10 for the AFC title on a frozen Three Rivers Stadium turf. I remember the jubilation we felt on becoming only the second AFC team in history to make back-to-back trips to the Super Bowl. But now we had the added burden of playing against the dreaded Dallas Cowboys in Super Bowl X.

I was scared to death of the Cowboys and didn't feel I was going to play well against them. For one thing, their flex defense was complex, hard to pick up on, and I knew that to beat them I would have to play one of my best games. Then there was the psychological factor. I'd never played well against the Cowboys. And, don't forget, back home in north Louisiana, the Dallas Cowboys were kings. They may have been America's team, but they were also Shreveport's team. So this game was important to me for lots of reasons, not the least of which was that I had to face the great Roger Staubach. The obvious comparisons between Bradshaw and Staubach were beginning to surface and, of course, I stood to lose in that.

I also hated the idea of facing the media barrage, because I knew I'd be asked how a stupid guy like me could get his team back to the Super Bowl. I remember locking myself in my room, never going out, and never reading the papers.

Frankly, I was sick of it. I kept thinking, "This is supposed to be the greatest game of the year and I'm not having any fun." I'd finally been voted to the Pro Bowl as a second-teamer and was beginning to gain some respect, but now I had to go through all this garbage with the media again. Even though I didn't read the papers, the press would repeat to me what all the Cowboys had said about me, most of which referred to my intelligence.

Furthermore, everybody was picking the Cowboys to win. They were still a glamour team, even if they weren't the best team in the Super Bowl.

The Cowboys had white-collar fans and represented the upper middle class. They were pure Hollywood, with those flashy silver and blue uniforms and a hole in the roof of their stadium (how come they never covered it up?). They had that fancy turf. Computerized scouting. Body fat testing. All that stuff that helps win football games, right?

Our guys were blue-collar and felt the Cowboys were soft. We were going to kick them and slap them around, intimidate them. Dwight "Mad Dog" White would knee you in the face when he tackled you. And then he'd cuss you and your mama. Mean Joe Greene would spit at you, take off your helmet, and beat you with it. L. C. "Hollywood Bags" Greenwood would body slam you. Jack "Fangs" Lambert would be foaming at the mouth as he lined up in front of the quarterback.

They all had one thing in common: they knew that to beat the Cowboys, you attack their pride and their heart. They knew that you can never let the Cowboys get the upper hand on you, so they didn't. Besides, we just plain didn't like the Cowboys. The Cowboys would never admit it, but I think we intimidated them. Not Staubach, because I don't think he could ever be intimidated. But I think the rest of them were.

Unfortunately, the "dumb" thing kept cropping up. It was the beginning of the comparison between Bradshaw, the small-college redneck, versus Staubach of the Naval Academy, Heisman Trophy winner. If they were going to compare me to Staubach and call me dumb because I couldn't get into the Naval Academy, then I was defenseless, because there was no way I could ever measure up to those credentials.

"Do you call your own plays, Terry?" the press would ask.

"Well, yes, I call my own plays."

"Man, are you kidding? You really call your own plays?"

"Yeah, man, I call my own plays. Yeah, do my own play calling. Go ahead, man, write that down."

I found it rather peculiar that the Cowboys should be talking so much trash and that everyone favored them. After all, they had barely beat the Vikings in the NFC semifinals, 17–14, on one of Staubach's Hail Mary passes, and were in the Super Bowl as a wild-card team.

It's funny what things make an impression on you about Super Bowls. My most vivid recollection of Super Bowl X is Tom Sullivan singing the national anthem. It was the most unbelievable rendition of the "Star-Spangled Banner" I had ever heard or have heard since. I met Tom years later and told him when he sang that day it was the most beautiful anthem I'd ever heard. I wanted him to know it.

It was a beautiful day—clear, sunny, not too hot. I remember looking up in the sky at the Goodyear Blimp. I didn't realize it at the time, but they were filming *Black Sunday*, with Robert Shaw. That was special. But like at all Super Bowls, I didn't feel the magnitude of the event until I stepped onto the field.

I remember looking around the Orange Bowl and seeing so much Steeler black and gold. We had great fans, tough fans—tough as our defense. They would take on the entire stadium and they followed us everywhere.

The Cowboys opened the game up with a double reverse and scored early on a play-action pass—Staubach hit Drew Pearson over the middle. Standing on the sideline, I said to myself, "We're going to lose this game."

I knew the way to play the Cowboys was to attack their deep secondary. I had planned to sacrifice the percentage pass and go for the bomb, because their defense was vulnerable to it. First, however, I had to take what the defense gave me. Although we came right back and I hit Randy Grossman on a play-action pass for a touchdown, my performance was very average, if not below average. Roger didn't play much better; he outplayed me but was getting knocked on his butt by our swarming defense. And he didn't have Lynn Swann. I did.

Swann was absolutely remarkable. He caught four passes for 161 yards, one of them for sixty-four yards and a touchdown. He *averaged* more than forty yards a catch. Lynn was rightly voted the game's Most Valuable Player.

This game would have everything. It was close, with some spectacular offensive plays. Both quarterbacks were harassed and sacked but made big throws. I only made two good throws all day. The rest were just great catches.

It was in this game I began to feel capable of rising to the elite status among NFL quarterbacks. I was ready to make that leap, ready to be recognized as one of the best, ready to be named MVP in a Super Bowl. I answered my critics by throwing for 209 yards—five more than Roger—and two touchdowns. Roger also had two TD passes.

I got knocked out by Larry Cole of the Cowboys on the sixty-four-yard touchdown pass to Swann, probably the best pass of my career. Swann never had to break stride. It wasn't a cheap shot by Cole, he just happened to catch me flush on the jaw. That tells you right there I could never be a boxer.

It still ranks as one of the best Super Bowls ever played and up to that point was *the* best. But it was not without controversy. Chuck elected to go for it on fourth down with very little time remaining, because he had no confidence in our punter, Bobby Walden, who had dropped a ball earlier. So on fourth down and nine at the Dallas forty-one yard line, with a minute and twenty-eight seconds left in the game, Chuck called a running play: Rocky Bleier off tackle for two yards. Short. We had given the ball back to the Cowboys with good field position, leading only by four points. Roger still had a chance to win it.

Super Bowl X ended with Roger throwing passes into our end zone, against the number-one defense in the NFL, trying to pull off one of those miraculous comebacks that made him famous. Glen Edwards intercepted a pass intended for Drew Pearson in the end zone and ran it back to the thirty-eight yard line at the gun.

I missed the exciting finish because I was out cold in the locker room, where I had been since hitting Swann with the touchdown pass with two minutes and two seconds left to play. That put us up 21–10. I figured that lead would be safe, but Staubach nearly pulled it out.

As I came to, I kept hearing a man's voice saying, "You did it, big guy! You did it, big guy!" and it sounded hundreds of miles away. I was stretched out in the locker room and when I woke up I was looking right in the face of Tom Brookshier of CBS. Not Farrah Fawcett or Kathleen Turner, but Tom Brookshier. Talk about a nightmare. Brookshier scared me to death. Then I heard the crowd yell and knew we had won the game. I didn't know until later, when my dad told me, that the pass I had thrown to Swann when I got knocked out by Larry Cole had gone for a touchdown.

Cole wound up doing me a favor. By knocking me out, he spared me from experiencing those last frightening eighty-two seconds. And better yet, I didn't have to go to the post-game press conferences and be asked if I thought I'd overcome my dumb image.

I spent the night with a bad headache from a concussion, throwing up everywhere. They put me in bed and I woke up around midnight, called my parents at their hotel, and they came by to pick me up. They took me to a party, but I only stayed for a short while because I was still groggy. And I was disappointed that because of the concussion I wouldn't be able to play in the Pro Bowl. Once again, no celebrating for old Terry. So I got on the plane with my family the next day and flew back to Louisiana.

SUPER BOWL XIII
Orange Bowl, Miami, Florida
January 21, 1979
Steelers 35, Cowboys 31

There really are two kinds of quarterbacks. One is struggling to become a contender, to make a name for himself and to convince his teammates to believe in themselves. That's most quarterbacks. The other is a defending champion everybody is gunning for, who is trying to excel when everybody is playing above their capabilities to stop him. After a two-year layoff from the championship game, we were trying to win our third Super Bowl in five years and it takes a certain kind of person to handle that pressure. It's a different kind of pressure from being a quarterback on a team that's not winning.

When you are a winner you hear people saying you can't do it again, your team can't repeat, and the majority of the sentiment goes to the other guys, the underdogs. To combat all that is a tremendous feeling of satisfaction. That's how I felt when we beat the Cowboys in XIII and I was voted MVP. This was my shining moment in all of sports. I was pumped up for this game and not afraid of playing against the Cowboys anymore. I'd just come off a season in which I was named the league's MVP and was at the top of my game.

The Steelers hadn't been in the Super Bowl for two years and were coming under fire from the press for being too old. We needed to make changes, but the players were motivated by all the criticism. They personally took upon themselves as a challenge to have our greatest year ever. And we did. That entire season was full of excitement. I was throwing the ball all over the field because we were among the first to take advantage of the liberalized rules that disallowed chucking a receiver more than once. Swann and Stallworth were making great catches. Franco was still getting his thousand yards. Rocky was contributing. The defense was overwhelming. And we were attacking with the pass on first down. We were throwing the ball more than thirty times a game and beating teams by big margins. As a result, I got a lot of rest because I sat out a lot of fourth quarters.

My confidence was soaring and I had more personal highs that season than any of my career. And in the first half of this game, I would play the best half of football I ever played in my life. But in the second half, I lost both Swann and Stallworth to injuries, and we had to hold on for dear life to hold off Roger Staubach.

To get there we destroyed Denver, the defending AFC champions, in the first round of the playoffs, 33–10. We annihilated Houston 34–5. Now I had a new kind of pressure as the big gun. It's different when you are along for the ride and aren't one of the team's stars. In Super Bowls IX and X, the Steelers depended on Franco and our defense. Through the entire season leading up to Super Bowl XIII, the team depended on me. I had to deliver. If I didn't play well, I knew we were going to lose. This was a totally new kind of pressure. Now all of a sudden I'm All-Pro, I'm the main guy the Cowboys have to stop. And I'm saying to myself, "Hey, wait a minute! I don't want to be the big gun! Freeze on the big gun. It's Franco! You guys gotta stop Franco, not me! I'm the dumb guy, remember?"

Dallas linebacker Hollywood Henderson remembered. He didn't waste any time—he went right for my brain. Now they were going to question whether I could spell. And I said to myself, "Hey, time out! I thought this dumb stuff had been laid to rest."

You think an image dies easily? Here we had already won two Super Bowls, including the victory over the Cowboys three years earlier, and that old "dummy" label pops up again. Here comes this clown they call Hollywood, looking for a little notoriety, trying to get a little press. If the Cowboys win the Super Bowl, he's going to be on every talk show, writing books, and starring in movies.

Sure enough, at the daily press conference in Miami before Super Bowl XIII, Thomas "Hollywood" Henderson told the media: "Bradshaw can't spell 'cat' if you spot him the 'c' and the 'a.' " Pretty funny line, to everybody exept me. I wasn't reading the papers that week and didn't know about Henderson's comment until reporters asked me about it. I, of course, made fun of it and said: "I can, too: C—A . . .T." I'd worked out a good relationship with the press, had been having fun with them, and now I had to start defending myself again. This was garbage. It only made matters more difficult for me, because when we arrived in Miami, I had other pressures: my marriage.

My wife, Jo Jo Starbuck, an ice skating star with the Ice Capades, had been performing in New York, and I hadn't seen her for a long time. She didn't care about football and didn't particularly want to come to the game, but I was trying to convince her to fly down to Miami. I'm coming off my greatest year, playing the biggest game of my career, having spent most of the year alone because my wife was traveling around the world ice skating, and on top of this I've got this clown Henderson insulting my intelligence.

And I was scared to death we were going to lose. Seems like I was always scared to death in Super Bowls, even when I was confident about my own ability, because you never know when it's going to be your last one, and you don't want your last one to be a losing effort. By winning XIII, the Steelers would become part of NFL history: the first team to ever win three. I wanted that with all my heart.

We were comfortable in Miami because we were prepared and we knew the turf. Our offense didn't change at all and we only had to study the application of it to the Cowboys' flex defense.

The night before the game I was kept awake by the noise around the pool—my room was right next to it. I changed rooms. Jo Jo finally arrived. She was tired and went right to bed. I woke up at four A.M. It was pouring down rain and it was blowing so hard I thought it was a hurricane. I could hear it but couldn't see it. I sat in a chair in front of the window, thinking about the game and what was going to happen in about twelve hours.

What's going to happen today, Terry? Are you going to play well? Are you going to match your performance of the playoffs? Can you throw deep on these guys? What if they blitz? What if they don't blitz? What if they fake the blitz? What are they going to do on first down? What are you going to do if you're behind? How are you going to respond to the fans? You're the main target and what if the Cowboys knock you out of the game?

I played games with my mind until well after dawn. And listened to the rain. At dawn I could see the palm trees swaying in the wind. All I could think was, "This is going to be great, the Orange Bowl field will be muddy! Who plays well on muddy fields? I do! Who throws a wet ball well? I do! What do you do when it's wet and muddy? Throw the football! What have we been doing all year? Throwing the football! How'd we beat Houston? In an icy rain with me throwing the ball all over the place!"

All of a sudden I was excited.

Wouldn't you know it? Somebody went out to that Orange Bowl and put a tarp on that field and it was drier than the Sahara Desert. It was what you call a fast track. My hopes for a muddy field went up in smoke, or in a tarp.

As I look back at all these Super Bowls, the most gratifying part of them was having my family there to share it with me. As always, the entire Bradshaw clan was there: my Aunt Margie Gay, Uncle "Duck" and Aunt Betty Gay, my mom and dad, my brothers Gary and Craig, Gary's wife Susan, my accountant and business manager, Gil Shanley, and my attorney, Gerald Burnett. About the only close member of my family who didn't come was my uncle Bobby Gay, who is like a brother to me. I'm close to Bobby and love him dearly. He runs the ranch for me in Grand Cane, and he just never felt he could leave the ranch long enough to go to a Super Bowl.

Super Bowl XIII was the most pressure-packed game I ever played in. The magnitude of the game had grown since we'd played in it. And our being heavy favorites just added more heat. On the bus ride to the game that day I noticed that there seemed to be more fans, although it couldn't have been any more than Super Bowl X at the Orange Bowl. The whole game just seemed bigger.

I got dressed quickly, got out my chewing gum and tobacco, threw my game plan in the garbage, and went over to play cards. I remember seeing the TV stands in the locker room for the postgame interviews and presentation of the Lombardi Trophy. It reminded me that this was a big game. There was a camera in the locker room always looking at you.

Super Bowl XIII will be remembered by Cowboy fans as

the one that got away. The one in which tight end Jackie Smith made the celebrated drop in the end zone. Although people have come to remember that drop by Smith as the deciding factor, it actually happened midway through the third quarter on third down and three at our ten yard line. It would have tied the game, but as it turned out the Cowboys got a Rafael Septien field goal out of it.

Jackie should have caught the ball—it was a sure touchdown pass—but I think he was fooled by Roger's motion. Staubach gave him the fastball look, but threw him a change-up. Smith was wide open, but he dropped the ball because he was girding to catch a hard throw and Roger took something off of it. Had Roger fired the football in there, Smith would have caught it. I've told Roger this and I think he agrees with me.

The Cowboys started out the game behind the running of Tony Dorsett but then did something that is very Cowboy-like: after making about ten yards a pop with Dorsett, Tom Landry called a trick play, a reverse throwback on which there was a muffed handoff. We recovered, drove down the field, and I threw a touchdown pass to Stallworth in the corner of the end zone.

It was another case of the Cowboys' Tom-foolery only fooling themselves.

We safety-blitzed Roger Staubach from the blind side, but he picked it up at the last second and threw a touchdown pass to Tony Hill: tied 7–7. Then Mike Hegman stole the ball from me as I was being tackled and ran it into the end zone; that made it 14–7. I landed on my shoulder and reinjured a nerve I'd hurt in training camp. My shoulder was in flames. Everybody was concerned but me. This was one game when I felt supremely confident from the beginning to the end. Nothing bothered me. I felt like I had them. This was the only game in my life I ever felt this way for the whole game. Even though over the next few years I played better, this was the only game in which I knew I was in total control of everything that happened on the field. It was eerie.

I threw a seventy-basic route to Stallworth, who took a

ten-yard pass and turned it into a seventy-five yard touch-down play. Then we went to the two-minute drill and drove fifty-six yards. I sprinted out and hit Rocky on a seven-yard swing pass for the touchdown. When you see that pass on film, it looks like I threw the ball behind him. But I was in complete control, and when you get that way, you can see everything. You have totally clear vision. There was no way I could lay the ball out for Rocky. He was heavily covered on the sideline, but there was space behind him, uncovered, and with nobody blitzing, I could lay the ball up softly and he could make the adjustment. And if he didn't, it was just incomplete and we could kick a field goal. I deliberately threw the ball behind him so he could turn around, because the defensive back was in front of him by a half step. That gave Rocky a half-step advantage and the touchdown.

At the end of the first half we were on top 21–14. I had completed eleven passes for 253 yards and three touch-downs in only two quarters. But the second half brought bad news: I lost my receivers. Stallworth had leg cramps. Swann played with an injury but had trouble holding the ball at times. We just ran the ball, played conservatively, and put the pressure on our defense.

With twelve minutes left to play in the game, we were ahead 21–17 when we went eighty-five yards for a touch-down, aided by a controversial tripping penalty that cost Dallas thirty-three yards. Field Judge Fred Swearingen made the call, and it was certainly questionable: Swann fell over Benny Barnes's ankles and it shouldn't have been a flag. Franco blasted nine yards off left guard for the score and we led 28–17.

My fourth touchdown pass came after Randy White fumbled the kickoff. I hit Swann on the back edge of the end zone for what would prove to be the winning score.

Late in the game some of our players started high-fiving and jumping up and down on the sidelines, and I got steamed, because I knew what kind of quarterback Stau-bach was. I'd played against him too many times and knew that if you relaxed on him, he'd beat you. You want to score as many points as you can and not let up, because if you do Staubach will kill you. We were ahead 35–17 and I could feel us let up. I remember screaming at them: "This isn't over!" Sure enough, the Cowboys rallied for two touchdowns in the last five minutes, both passes by Staubach, and all they needed was an onside kick recovery and a touchdown to win the game. Only when Rocky recovered Septien's onside kick did I start to breathe again.

The Steelers beat the Cowboys 35–31 in Super Bowl XIII, and even though it shut Henderson's mouth, the quote stuck. I wonder how many people remember that remark more than the fact that I threw for four touchdown passes and was named the game's MVP. I was ecstatic. A storybook finish to a dream season. My father and brothers were in the postgame interviews and my brother tossed me my pouch of Red Man chewing tobacco.

When reporters approached Henderson after the game and asked him what he thought of my performance, according to the account by Phil Musick of the *Post-Gazette*, Henderson told them: "I was rating his intelligence, not his ability." But Henderson's comment couldn't rob me of my joy. I honestly felt I had finally joined the elite among NFL quarterbacks after winning my third Super Bowl. I had proven myself, completing seventeen passes for 318 yards and four touchdown passes. Those four TD passes, I'm proud to say, still stand as a Super Bowl record.

At last, a chance to celebrate in a Super Bowl victory party. About eighteen members of my family drank champagne and celebrated. We played cards and laughed until dawn. I didn't want that night to ever end. There is nothing worse than not having anyone to share your success with, and I'm happy to say that in my greatest moments as an athlete, my folks were there with me. The best feeling I had was walking into my hotel suite and getting a standing ovation from my family. I get goose bumps just thinking about it.

But I'll tell you how short-lived it was: the following week in the Pro Bowl, I got ripped by the media for having a bad game.

SUPER BOWL XIV
Rose Bowl, Pasadena, California
January 20, 1980
Steelers 31, Rams 19

I don't remember a great deal about the 1979 season, only that it wasn't quite as good as the year before. I threw more interceptions, but I threw a lot of touchdown passes. I had a good season, but the pressure was on to perform well every game. You make a name for yourself, you've got to live up to it.

Our archrival had been the Raiders; now it was the Oilers. The Oilers had beaten us on the next-to-last game of the season, 20–17, on a Monday night game in the Astrodome; they were the one team I feared that year. Bum Phillips remarked that the Oilers had been knocking on the door the year before, but this year they were "going to knock it down." But after beating Miami in the first round, 34–14, we won the AFC title on a close game with Houston, 27–13.

We had been the first team to win three Super Bowls, and now we were trying to be the first team to win them back-to-back twice, to win four titles in six years. It seemed like there was always another carrot dangling out there to chase. Naturally, it was an emotional time for us, but there was a certain mental fatigue that was taking its toll. Odd as it may seem, I was still afraid of blowing it, of missing out on this chance to make history. And it seemed the pressure was greater than ever.

The off-season money had started to roll in after winning Super Bowl XIII. I hadn't made a dime after the first two Super Bowls, but after XIII people started to call—that's the bonus for a good season. It was even more important in those days, before pro football players starting making big money. I probably made more than half of my salary the year before in speaking engagements and appearances. My salary was $250,000, and altogether with my appearances and my role in *Cannonball Run*, I knocked down another $150,000.

But it cost me in other ways. You work hard all your life to become a champion and when you get there, you almost resent the fact that people only love you if you're a winner. You finally say, "This is what I wanted, but this is more than I wanted."

If I had the choice between going on the road and making five thousand bucks or staying home and working out, I'd go on the road. This was all new to me and the financial reward was enticing. Jo Jo was traveling, too, so we hardly saw each other. I was committed to trying to make some serious cash, and she was committed to ice skating. Right there you can see trouble was ahead.

Truthfully, I didn't work out much in the off-season and didn't even give the season much thought until around July. I knew it was a special year for us—when we reached training camp at Latrobe, we had 15,000 fans for picture day and practices were always packed. Practice became showtime, and you tried to perform a little better than usual. But then Chuck shut it down and turned the fans away, so it got quiet in a hurry.

Super Bowl XIV was different from any I'd experienced. We could no longer dominate with our defense, and if I didn't play well, we didn't win. The game had changed: there was no more mugging of receivers off the line of scrimmage; it was more of a quarterback's era.

For me, it was a tough year emotionally. My marriage was on the rocks, we were going through a divorce, and so I turned most of my attention to football, but there was more pressure than ever for me to perform. I was a miserable person but a pretty good quarterback, because I played well almost every week.

Anyway, we beat my friend Bum Phillips again and went to California to play the Rams, who were 9–7 on the season and really didn't deserve to be there. Vince Ferragamo was the Rams' quarterback and, much like me in my first Super Bowl, hadn't even been a starter most of the regular season.

Our dynasty was starting to fade, or so they said. We were supposed to blow out these Rams, because they had gotten to the Super Bowl by beating the Cowboys on a deflected pass. But what the critics didn't take into account was that the Steelers had scrambled to a 12–4 record and were no cinch against anybody.

The worst week of my life was spent in Los Angeles. There was a movie out called *Heaven Can Wait*, starring Warren Beatty, who always dreamed of being a quarterback and playing in a big game but was killed. His guardian angel put him in the body of a quarterback—a Rams quarterback. They play in the Super Bowl against—guess who?—the Pittsburgh Steelers. He runs for a touchdown, beats the Steelers, and becomes a hero. They played this movie over and over again in our hotel and, of course, I watched it, and I am saying, "This is an omen! We are going to lose this game. This is an omen!"

I was doing a psyche job on myself. My wife was causing me problems, driving me crazy. My family was there and that's nice, but I'm trying to concentrate on this game and this is a terrible week.

I was so nervous the night before the game I couldn't sleep a lick. And then when I did fall asleep, I missed chapel service that morning of the game and to me that was a no-no. I had people calling me for tickets, all of my so-called friends that I hear from once a year, and to top all this off, the defensive coach of the Rams is Bud Carson, the guy who helped shape the Steel Curtain in Pittsburgh. The Rams' offensive line coach was Dan Radokovich, formerly of the Steelers. They knew our offense, our defense, our adjustments. They knew where we wanted to trap, how we wanted to trap, when we would pull, when we wouldn't. It was like looking in the mirror and playing against yourself.

I said, "Holy cow! How do you beat yourself?" Or, how do you keep from beating yourself?

You gotta beat them with talent and execution. You gotta

get lucky, and we did. I promptly went out and threw three interceptions.

The Rams dropped a pass in the end zone that could have killed us. We were behind at halftime, 13–10. Then I beat the blitz and hit Swann with a forty-seven yard touchdown pass. Beautiful catch by Swann—he could jump like nothing you've ever seen. The Rams kept coming back. They connected on a halfback option pass to take the lead, 19–17, and now it's the fourth quarter and time for heroics.

Chuck had this play, sixty-prevent slot hook and go, with Stallworth in the slot. I didn't like the play because it took too long to develop, and I didn't want to run it. But Chuck called me to the sideline on third down and eight yards to go at our own twenty-seven and said, "They're not going to give us anything short, so we have to go deep to beat these guys. You can do it!" The Rams blew the coverage, but Stallworth's man was with him all the way. I just laid the ball up and the defensive back swiped at it, barely missing. Stallworth made the catch and went all the way, seventy-three yards, and we took the lead, 24–19.

But it wasn't over. The Rams were driving at our thirty-two yard line and the crowd at the Rose Bowl was going nuts when Lambert intercepted Ferragamo with just over five minutes left. We had to do something. So we went back to sixty-prevent slot hook and go. By now I'm starting to like this play.

On third and seven at our own thirty-three, I put the ball up and Stallworth made this unbelievable over-the-head, diving catch that I still can't believe whenever I see it on film. One of the great catches in Super Bowl history. Franco scored from the one and we won it big, 31–19, but the game was much closer than the score indicated.

I never had a bit of confidence in that game, and if it hadn't been for Swann and Stallworth, I'd have had a very mediocre performance. Swann made a touchdown catch on a ball that shouldn't have been caught at all. Stallworth made two beautiful catches—his miracle grab for the score bailed me out. I looked like a hero, but the true MVP of that game was Stallworth. I'm not sure why the writers and broadcasters voted me the Most Valuable Player, unless it was because they were paying tribute to the fact that I had quarterbacked four Super Bowl winners.

I went to the team party that night, my first one, but didn't stay long. I came back and played cards with my family. I didn't even go to bed because I had committed to go on "Good Morning America" with David Hartman at 3:30 A.M.

It took me two months to mentally get back to the game after winning Super Bowl XIV. You get so much adulation, so many pats on the back, that it starts to drive you crazy. And the breakup of my marriage was weighing heavily on my mind and heart. My wife was going on a tour somewhere, and by then I just wanted her to go as far away as possible.

The MVP trophies from Super Bowls XIII and XIV were the only trophies that ever meant anything to me. We got rings, but you couldn't take the Super Bowl trophy home with you. What that MVP trophy means is that in the biggest game of the year, you excelled. In Super Bowl XIII I deserved to be MVP because I threw four touchdown passes. In Super Bowl XIV, I didn't. Even though I threw touchdown passes of seventy-three yards to Stallworth and forty-seven yards to Swann, I also threw three interceptions, which is something I rarely did in big games.

Even though the nine touchdown passes I've thrown in Super Bowls are a record, I have to confess that a large part of that success can be attributed to Swann's and Stallworth's abilities, and another large part to just plain luck. And that's not intended to be false modesty. Nor will I concede to my critics who say, "Bradshaw was just along for the ride," because clearly there were times when I was behind the wheel. I just think it's only fair to point it out when other people play a part in your success. I'm prepared to receive credit when it is due, but I'm also prepared to give it.

10

THE DAY THEY OPERATED ON THE ELBOW OF "THOMAS BRADY"

There were times when I found it difficult to be motivated, especially when I could sense my teammates had lost their passion for winning. By the fall of 1980 the Steelers had done it all—four Super Bowl titles in six years—so what else was there to achieve in football? I could see signs of lethargy during the season following Super Bowl XIV.

We played San Diego at the end of the 1980 season, and when I saw some of my teammates giving a half-assed effort, I was so appalled that I almost wanted to quit right after the game. We just didn't seem to care if we beat the Chargers, and we didn't. We lost the game 26–17 and wound up with a record of 9–7, breaking a string of eight straight playoff appearances. I saw something in my old teammates that I never thought I'd see: suddenly they didn't seem to care about winning anymore—or so I thought. That took a lot out of me. I wanted to tell them to kiss off, walk out of there, and never come back.

But to be honest, I, too, had had difficulty keeping interested some days, and the fire in my belly had begun to flicker. If Chuck Noll were totally honest, he would admit the same thing. I can recall playing in a game where I said to myself: "H-m-m-m. Where's the thrill here? Hold it! Something's missing." Like Peggy Lee sings, "Is that all there is?"

For instance, I always hated playing in Buffalo. Number one, it was usually forty below zero. And number two, the Bills were always fired up and trying to kick our butts. Everybody wanted to beat the Steelers because we were Top Guns, and had to keep proving ourselves. One year I felt like walking up to Chuck and saying: "Excuse me, Chuck, can I have a word with you? I realize this is the tenth game of the season and we are coming down the home stretch, but I really don't feel like playing today." I can just see Chuck's face turning into a furnace. Some days I felt like throwing in the towel, but I never did. The professional athlete knows if he ever admits to something like that his stock would not only fall with the coach but with the fans as well. Yet, I'll bet every single pro athlete has had days, or nights, like that.

Obviously, not every athlete is motivated every day or night, especially in the NBA, with eighty-two regular-season games, or in major league baseball, with 162. But in the NFL we only play sixteen and that doesn't seem to be asking too much. I realize that with the addition of the Hall of Fame preseason game in Canton, Ohio, the American Bowl in London, four other preseason games, sixteen regular-season games, the wild card game, playoffs, Super Bowl, and Pro Bowl, it's possible for some players to play twenty-six games in a single season, which is incredible. But that's rarely going to happen.

Still, whether athletes admit it or not, it's difficult for the better teams to get up for the Green Bay Packers or San Diego Chargers, or maybe even the Pittsburgh Steelers. Otherwise, teams like the Giants and Bears would have been able to repeat as Super Bowl champions, which they did not. The Steelers teams I played on had a remarkable resiliency. We were able to stay motivated for a longer period than most teams. We never got fat during that six-year period and that's probably why we were able to achieve greatness. But not without a price. The pressure of those Super Bowls carries over season to season. I was always scared to death we were going to lose and it seemed to get more frightening every time we went to another Super Bowl. Sooner or later, everybody runs out of adrenaline.

Just as Jack Nicklaus planned each of his golf seasons around the four major championships—the Masters, U.S. Open, British Open, and PGA—we got up for Super Bowls. Nicklaus realized at an early age he needed to target his goals. Winning the Buick Open and the Quad Cities Open were not high on his list of priorities, so he didn't try to fake it. After twenty major championships, however, you've pretty much done it all.

In a way, that's what happened to the Steelers. We got older and eventually it got harder for us to concentrate. Sometimes the Steelers just couldn't get up for a regular season game in Buffalo. There is also a wear-and-tear factor on your body in football, of course; that's not as much of a problem in other sports. You don't usually realize the toll until you reach middle age. And there is the wear-and-tear factor on your brain, which in my case was related to Chuck Noll.

The people from a TV production company approached me at that point and made an offer for me to star in a series called "Stockers" with Mel Tillis, my country-music-star friend, and the offer sounded incredible. Here was a chance to make more money than I could for the remainder of my football career.

When you have to make a decision like that, you look to justify it in your mind. In my case, I just couldn't get excited about playing Buffalo, Houston, Cleveland, Cincinnati, and all those teams who would be laying in the weeds for us. So I rolled the dice and signed the contract to do "Stockers" with Mel. That summer before training camp started I announced to the press that if the pilot was successful and the series was picked up by NBC, my football career was over.

Naturally, Chuck was upset with me. The whole city of Pittsburgh was mad because they felt I was deserting them.

We had brought some fame and fortune to a city that deserved it, an owner and a management team that deserved it, an organization that deserved it. I felt I had helped bring some pride back to Pittsburgh. Now I wanted to think about myself for a change. Here was a chance to make some money and move back to the South.

"Stockers" was no fly-by-night operation. It was a Johnny Carson Production, and I was working with two great people: Albert Ruddy, who had won an Oscar for *The Godfather*, and Hal Needham, director of *Cannonball Run*. As you might guess, "Stockers" was NBC's answer to "The Dukes of Hazzard": a story about two redneck stock-car drivers. Both Ruddy and Needham thought this thing was going to be a smash hit.

Mel Tillis is one of the funniest people on the face of the earth. One of the reasons that we wound up doing this pilot is that when Mel and I worked together in *Cannonball Run*, people seemed to think we had a special chemistry. Ruddy and Needham felt Mel and I were so funny together that we ought to have had a larger part in the movie. Instead, we got a chance to make our own series.

It seemed like the filming of "Stockers" was going so well. We had more than two hundred people around the set every day, and they were constantly laughing. The stuff was hilarious. It was good, and I was proud of my acting. All the guys in suits were telling Mel and me that we were terrific. And all of a sudden, it turned cold. To this day, I don't know why.

The trouble started when they cut the pilot to thirty minutes. It was aired while I was playing in a golf tournament in Montgomery, Alabama, with, of all people, Ernest Borgnine. I had invited Ernest up to the room to watch "Stockers." But when I saw it, I was so embarrassed I could have jumped out the window. Ernest tried to console me. He said, "You have nothing to be ashamed of, Terry, it was just poorly done. You and Mel have chemistry together, and what you need is the right project." The man was so damned nice.

The phone rang in my room and I heard this guy on the other end trying to talk. It was Mel.

"Ah, ah, T-t-t-terry!" Mel blurted out.

"Hello, Mel! What did you think?"

"It s-s-s-sure wasn't *Gone with the Wind.*"

That was the end of "Stockers." It needed to draw a twenty-two share and got only about a fourteen, although we got some pretty good reviews. I regretted it, because it's something I would love to have pursued. I can imagine how unhappy Chuck was about my threatening to retire in '81. It probably led to some of our difficulties in the next few seasons. But I said to myself: what's next? And I couldn't find the answer within myself. What was going to be next was a couple of years of football and then a new career in the business of being a celebrity.

You should never try to make friends with your head coach. Don't think the guy really likes you, because he doesn't. Chuck Noll and I never had a genuine friendship, as it turned out—just a working relationship. When my job was over, so was our relationship. It all began to fester that day back in March of 1983 when I checked into Doctor's Hospital in Shreveport, Louisiana, under the name of "Thomas Brady" and had my right elbow operated on by Dr. Bill Bundrick.

Some people have criticized my decision to have a hometown surgeon operate on my right arm, but Dr. Bundrick had enjoyed amazing success with this type of operation and, besides, the elbow was killing me. If I was going to have surgery, I felt my chances were better with my personal physician, who took an interest in my well-being. I thought I'd be completely healed by that fall, but the rehab took longer and I missed virtually the entire 1983 season, with the exception of my cameo appearance against the Jets.

Obviously, Chuck was unhappy with me. He didn't even want me around the team during the '83 season—not at practice, not on the sideline, not in the press box, not anywhere.

When you are injured, you are made to feel you do not belong anymore. You no longer exist. No one talks to you. No one asks you how you're doing. No one calls you. That's why players hate being hurt—if you're injured, you can't contribute, and if you don't contribute, you're not part of the team. If you can't produce, they don't recognize your existence. Terry who? Franco who? That's why athletes play hurt, why they take shots of novocaine, and why they're willing to risk permanent injury. Isolation from the team is the one thing football players fear most of all, because it's an early sign of things to come when you can no longer play. It's survival of the fittest and there is no place for the weak or infirm.

I'm a good-sized fellow, 6'3" and 210, and I never had a knee operation in my life. But there are times when my body hurts all over, even today. My legs hurt, my knee hurts, my shoulder aches, and I have severe back pain from breaking my neck against the Cleveland Browns when Joe "Turkey" Jones body-slammed me to the ground. I don't consider it a cheap shot, however, because it wasn't premeditated—he just got caught up in the crowd noise and excitement of the game. In the mid '70s the NFL didn't have the "in-the-grasp" rule, which means that the officials blow the whistle when one or more defensive players have a grip on the quarterback. This rule was designed to keep quarterbacks from becoming cannon fodder—one defender standing the quarterback up while others take cheap shots at him, or the tackler simply tossing the quarterback around like a rag doll.

I suffered a serious back injury, a broken vertebra, when "Turkey" Jones tried to strike oil with my head. To this day, my neck stiffens up on me, and I get tremendous pain in my upper spine. My injury was one of the incidents that led to the creation of the "in-the-grasp" rule. Yet, personally, I think it's a bad rule, because it penalizes the great athletes like John Elway of the Broncos or Randall Cunningham of the Eagles, both of whom are strong enough to break the grasp of tacklers. No matter how many rules they pass, pain is always going to be a way of life for football players. I've broken bones, dislocated shoulders, cracked vertebrae, and suffered more concussions than most prize fighters, but the worst part of football is not the pain. The worst part is the fear of being permanently injured. You can live with a certain amount of pain, but when the body malfunctions and you can't perform, it's frightening.

There are times in your career when the pain is so excruciating that you need relief. That's when they bring out the needles. It's not always the team doctor or the coach who wants you to shoot your elbow or foot or toe with novocaine. Sometimes the players ask for it without the knowledge of the coach. You will usually take any little edge you can get in your final years, although I drew the line at amphetamines and stimulants. I did, however, opt for the needle on several occasions, as do most players. Toward the end of my career, I had my elbow shot up regularly, and that only complicated matters. All the cortisone shots I took eventually turned my elbow muscles into mush and forced me to have surgery. Oddly enough, my elbow is completely healed and doesn't hurt anymore, but my body aches in other places—mostly the neck. What ended my career, however, was the elbow injury.

It started as a microscopic tear of the muscle in my right arm and felt like a strain. I hurt it in practice during the 1982 season, throwing a heavy, rain-soaked football. I'll never forget it: I looked to my right, threw to my left, and saw the ball come out sideways. I felt the sting and walked off the field holding my elbow. For the next few days, the pain came and went, like a nagging toothache. Finally I asked for novocaine.

The Steelers were going to Knoxville, Tennessee, in the summer of 1982 for an exhibition game. As I warmed up the day before, the elbow was killing me. I got so scared I went to the team doctor just before the game and asked him for a shot. I didn't want Chuck to know about it, so I asked the doctor to administer the pain-killer inside one of the cubicles of the men's room at the stadium. The two of us sneaked away from the field and hid inside the men's room, like a couple of junkies. What I didn't know was that it would deaden my ulna nerve, as the novocaine went all the way down my forearm and into my fingers. Imagine my shock when I returned to the field, reached down to grab the football and was unable to grip it—couldn't even get my fingers open. When I got up the nerve to tell Chuck, he looked at me with great dismay and asked, "What's the matter?" I was embarrassed to tell him I'd had my elbow shot up, because he didn't even know I'd hurt my elbow. After all, I was thirty-four years old then and in charge of my own body, so I didn't see the need to tell him about the injury. If I needed something done, I just did it without consulting anybody.

I can see now that maybe that was the beginning of the end of my career, because it led to my decision to have surgery, from which I never recuperated. All during the 1982 season my elbow was killing me. But after the second game, in which we beat Cincinnati, the players' strike hit and we didn't have another game for fifty-seven days. While I was down in Louisiana, I went to my doctor because I'd attempted to throw and the pain was still killing me. He said I had a muscle tear and that I could either play or have a simple operation to fix it. So I went back to Pittsburgh when the strike ended, had my elbow shot up every week, and played. We were 6–3 for the strike-shortened season and were eliminated by San Diego in the first round of the AFC playoffs. I went back to Shreveport and had Dr. Bundrick operate on my elbow.

I never actually told Chuck to his face that I planned to do this, but the Steelers knew. My business manager, Gil Shanley, and Dr. Bundrick had been in contact with Dan Rooney, trainer Ralph Berlin, and Dr. Paul Steele, the Steelers' orthopedic surgeon. Gil said he had asked that Dr. Bundrick communicate with Dr. Steele prior to surgery and describe the operation in medical terms. We sent them a Mailgram stating that I was to be operated on by Dr. Bundrick, unless the Steelers organization objected, in which case I would fly to Pittsburgh and be operated on by Dr. Steele. Gil also was in contact with Dennis Thimons, controller for the Steelers.

They gave permission for Dr. Bundrick to do the surgery. It came out later that they were unaware of it, which is a lot of crap. They knew the exact day of my surgery. They hedged and dragged their feet until it was too late to do anything. Then when I didn't rehab right away and couldn't play, they got mad. So there was ample time for the Steelers to intervene if they had so chosen. Of course, had I been able to see into the future, I would have done it differently, but I was led to think it was a simple operation with a short rehab.

Eventually my elbow did heal, but I tried to come back too early and paid for it with a premature retirement at thirty-five. Today, many athletes are playing into their late thirties and, except for my elbow, I was in good enough physical condition to keep on going.

You can imagine, then, how unhappy Chuck was when I reported for training camp in the summer of 1983 and was unable to play. We had words. Serious words. Then he tried a different approach. He would come into my room during training camp in Latrobe, and we'd laugh, play the guitar, and everything seemed okay. Chuck would say: "Why did you get this thing operated on? You threw the ball great last year." And I'd say, "Chuck, I know I threw it great, but my elbow hurt constantly." I sensed Chuck's frustration and began to feel the pressure from him.

It's not easy to hear your coach questioning your manhood and expressing disappointment in you. The insinuation is that you're faking it. Coaches play on the insecurity of athletes who are afraid there's some guy on the bench ready to take their job. Players are constantly reminded of Wally Pipp, the New York Yankee first baseman who took a day off because of a headache and never got his job back from Lou Gehrig. And as successful as I had been I never assumed that my job was safe. Chuck knew that fear motivated me, forced me to try to remain sharp. So Chuck—and even Dan Rooney—would say to me, "You've played with pain before." And I was trying to explain to them I couldn't throw the football. But I was trying hard to rehabilitate, lifting weights every day, even though I couldn't practice.

The Steelers decided their doctor should speed up the healing process, so he went in with a needle and ground away at the scar tissue; I guess that's supposed to stimulate the blood flow. I had to take off a week, and it still wasn't getting any better.

By then the season had started. In 1983, the Steelers lost three straight after winning nine of the first eleven games. Chuck was trying to be supportive of Cliff Stoudt, my replacement, and apparently thought my presence was a detriment to his progress. So I stayed home for the games, didn't even stand on the sideline, because that's what Chuck wanted. He didn't want the fans hollering "We want Bradshaw" every time Cliff threw an interception. He was very protective of Cliff. I was scared to death my career was over and could see that Chuck was gaining confidence in Cliff, that he wanted him to succeed. I felt worthless and was experiencing tremendous pressure to play. This is how cruel it gets: my own roommate, an offensive lineman, said to Walt Evans, the Steelers' strength coach, who was helping me get over my elbow injury, "Why are you helping that guy?" Suddenly I was considered an outsider.

While I was at home in Shreveport during my recovery period, I started working with this new rehab machine that Dr. Bundrick had begun using. At the first sign of improvement, I became ecstatic. I was ready to suit up and play right then. I left the doctor's office and went out on Hearne Avenue in Shreveport, with traffic heavy on both sides, to see if I could throw the football. Here I was, alongside a main thoroughfare, throwing passes.

After a couple of weeks, I was throwing the football with velocity. No pain. That convinced me to buy one of those fabulous machines. I paid twelve-thousand bucks for one so I could take it back to Pittsburgh with me for daily treatment. I even taught Walt how to use it. He'd give me treatment during the day and at night we'd open up the gym and throw the football. Things were looking up. The old racehorse with the broken leg was mending and, having escaped almost certain retirement, was coming back to the track to run again.

We were in a dogfight with Cleveland for the AFC Central Division title. The Steelers lost three games straight and began to slide. The heat was on Chuck and Cliff. The press was starting to close in on them. Every day the beat writers would ask about my physical condition.

That week in practice I must have completed everything I threw. So Chuck activated me. I knew early in the week before we were to play the Jets in New York that I was going to start, but I couldn't say anything. Finally, it came out that I was the starter.

Two days before this crucial game against New York, I was warming up and I felt the pain. My elbow was killing me and I was scared to death. Absolutely distraught. If I went to Chuck and told him I couldn't play, it would make Chuck look bad and put me in a terribly embarrassing position. It would have made the Steelers look like fools.

I didn't know what to do. I told Walt Evans about my pain and he gave me treatments all night, but I didn't say anything to Chuck. So the show went on and the next day when I went on the field at Shea Stadium, the pain was excruciating. Here the Steelers are in this huge game against the Jets with a sore-armed quarterback and the coach doesn't even know it.

But if the gamblers would have had inside information about my injury and tried to capitalize on it by betting on New York, they would have lost their shirts. By the grace of God I was able to take the team on a drive, throwing a touchdown pass across the field to Gregg Garrity. But I felt something snap; I looked down and my elbow was swollen. All I wanted to do was go somewhere and lie down and weep. The pain was unbelievable, but I couldn't let anyone know.

At the end of the first quarter we got the ball back, and I drove them down the field again. It was all I could do to get the ball to Calvin Sweeney over the middle, and he caught it for a touchdown. My last pass in football was for a touchdown to my old friend Sweeney, but when I look at the films of that play now, I can see that the ball almost went end over end and was about to hit the ground when Calvin caught it.

It was not a pretty sight. But we were ahead 14–0 and I came out.

I hadn't played all season because of a torn elbow muscle. After throwing two touchdown passes in fifteen minutes and forty-four seconds, I left the field for the last time— clutching my right elbow. Deep down, I knew it was over for me. No more surgery. No more shooting up the elbow with novocaine as I'd done so many times before. I simply couldn't throw the football anymore. The elbow would heal in time, but time wasn't something I had anymore. We beat the Jets 34–7 and clinched another AFC Central Division title. The following week we lost to Cleveland, but it didn't matter. My season was over and the Steelers were in the playoffs. Cliff played well against the Raiders, but we were eliminated, 38–10.

Now it was decision time for me. I pretty much sensed my career was over but gave it one more shot. After the season the press kept asking if I was going to play again. Chuck knew I wasn't, but he kept the press guessing, and maybe deep down he had the feeling that during the off-season I might rest the arm and get well. So the Steelers flew me out to California to have Dr. Frank Jobe, the world's leading authority on knees and elbows, examine me. He gave me one simple test with his hands, a little pressure check. He looked at me and said, "You have two options. You can build it up with weights or I'll operate on it, and you'll need a year and a half to recover. Then maybe you'll be able to play and maybe you won't." Here I was thirty-five and that would have brought me to thirty-seven, having missed at least another full year. So I opted for the weights.

That next May in minicamp I began to get big and strong from lifting. Then on one cool day I went out and threw a couple of passes. I felt the pain again and I walked right off the field and into the weight room. Chuck came in the weight room, and I said, "Chuck, that's it. I can't play any-more. It's over." He shook my hand and I left for my apart-ment. When I got there I just sat down and sobbed. Bawled my eyes out. One of those brokenhearted cries. I packed my stuff and left, but I didn't announce my retirement for another month.

I had signed with CBS and decided to make the announcement in New York. Joe Gordon, then the publicity man for the Steelers, wanted me to announce it in Pittsburgh, but I didn't want to make any fuss about it. That was my style. Honestly, I didn't feel I could have gone to Pittsburgh and announced my retirement without having an emotional breakdown. I couldn't stand up there in front of my friends and the writers I'd come to like and respect and completely fall apart. I just couldn't have done it, although that's the way most players do it. Right or wrong, that's the way it had to be.

When I was thirty-five years old, my playing days were over. When Chuck said I needed to "get on with my life's work"—as stinging a comment as it may have been—he was right, although I didn't want to hear it that way. He actually did me a favor by saying it.

Separation from the game is painful, even when you think you're emotionally ready for it, which I really wasn't that spring day of 1984 when I hung up jersey number twelve. After 25 years—fourteen seasons in the pros, four years in college, three years of high school, and a season in junior high—suddenly I was without football.

To this day, I've only been back to Three Rivers Stadium once—to do a promotional spot for KDKA-TV. I returned briefly in August 1987—I didn't even stay for the game—and began to reflect on the remarkable achievements of the Pittsburgh Steelers in the 1970s. I caught myself daydreaming, remembering my first touchdown pass as a Steeler, in 1970. I gazed down at the corner of the end zone where Ronnie Shanklin had caught the ball for a fifty-six-yard touchdown, the first touchdown pass ever thrown in brand-new Three Rivers Stadium. It gave me a warm feeling. But when you're standing on the field in street clothes, it's not the same as being in uniform.

Suddenly I realized I didn't belong there anymore. It was prior to kickoff and only a smattering of the crowd was in place. As I walked off the field I heard a few cheers, a few boos, and the warm feeling quickly subsided. Despite all the great moments at Three Rivers Stadium, the nostalgic moment evaporated and it was like being in any one of twenty-eight NFL stadiums. It didn't feel like home to me. These feelings aren't related in any way to the fans—I still have a great affection toward them. The city of Pittsburgh was a special place for me, despite my early years as an alien from Louisiana.

I guess I rode off in the sunset without ever saying goodbye to Pittsburgh. I don't blame anybody for what happened at the end. My own competitive nature and the fear of losing my job proved to be my undoing. I had come into the league with a gun for an arm and when I could no longer pull the trigger, it was finished.

There should be real concern for the athlete's mental and physical state when he leaves the game. Some people suggest that the National Football League Players Association ought to be spending more time negotiating retirement income, family counseling, and medical benefits for former players than pushing for higher salaries for current ones. Maybe so. To me, however, it's far more important that the player develop some kind of support system outside of football while he is playing so that when it's over, his whole world doesn't come crashing down on his head. He needs to be loved and supported emotionally. If he can't do anything but dig a ditch, his wife ought to say to him: "I love you. Dig the best ditch you can dig." But if that player has built his support group around other athletes and has married a groupie, then he is in trouble when it all ends.

What emotionally destroys an ex-athlete is when someone says: "You mean you're a ditch digger? Didn't you used to play for the New York Giants?" All of a sudden he's a failure. What that player needs is for someone to say: "Man, it's great to see you." It seems that society is too concerned with judging a person based on how he or she makes a living. So an athlete can't feel successful unless he's considered a "Mr. All-Pro Businessman."

If I wasn't doing what I'm doing now—working for CBS and making public appearances—I'd probably be a welder. Thank God I'm now married to a woman who tells me how proud she is of me. And I won't be judged by the kind of car I drive or the size of the house I live in. My kids will love me because I'm Daddy. And Daddy is going to work his tail off to take care of them.

Everybody knows I married Melissa Babitch, Miss Teenage America, shortly after arriving in Pittsburgh. I was introduced to her by another former Miss Teenage America, Debbie Patton of Odessa, Texas, when I was twenty and she was seventeen. When I first saw her, I was struck by her beauty, and evidently I confused that for love. The marriage lasted only eight months. It wasn't Melissa's fault; it was mine. I knew before I walked down the aisle that day that I didn't love her, but I wasn't man enough to admit it. So I did what I thought was right and went ahead with the marriage, which was foolish on my part because I was too immature to own up to my true feelings. I felt terrible about what I'd done. But I'm glad to know that Melissa is happily married now with several children, living in Alabama. And I wish her nothing but the best.

It's critical for these athletes to be loved by their families. Their value to their communities should not be measured by how many dollars they bring in.

Football players today don't have to work that hard for their money. They don't play two ways. There are specialists for kicking, specialists for catching passes on third down, specialists for short yardage, specialists for long yardage, specialists for stopping the short and long yardage—football has more specialists today than the Mayo Clinic has. Because of TV, they're like rock musicians: major stars making major dollars.

Just as the players in my era weren't as tough as the guys in the '50s and '60s, the players in the '80s and '90s aren't going to be as tough as they were in my day. Money has a way of curbing hunger in an athlete and making him mentally soft. For instance, watch a young free agent trying to make the team in training camp. Observe his work habits.

Then three years after he makes the team, watch that same player in training camp. He's a star now. Watch how he holds out for a new contract. Before, he would play with almost any kind of injury; now he's reluctant to go in the game with a hangnail. Gotta make that career last longer and make more money. When he first started, the simple thought of making it in the NFL was the overriding factor. Once he becomes established, he thinks he has earned the right to put forth less effort.

I'm not one of those old fogies who is going to sit around and complain that life dealt me a bad hand because I was born too soon, but I do think our sense of values has been warped by these incredible salaries. The big money began flowing just as I was leaving the game. When John Elway came into the NFL making a million dollars a season as a rookie in 1983, I was making a third of that after helping win four Super Bowls. Five years later Elway is making a million and a half a year, not even including a signing bonus that put him over two million. That's fine, because Elway has proven himself to be among the best players in the league. Nothing against John, but I just don't know whether any player is worth that kind of money. And I won't even go into the ridiculous salaries of baseball players such as Orel Hershiser and Frank Viola.

Maybe I'm blind. But if they're making two million a season now, what will kids be making ten years from now? But, hey, I don't want to sound like I'm jealous. Every generation tends to be critical of those who follow behind. I guess if Johnny Unitas and those guys were playing for twenty-five and thirty thousand in their prime, my three hundred thousand looked ludicrous to them. I just wonder if ten years from now today's players will be saying: "Eight million dollars a year? These guys are crazy to pay these kids that kind of money!"

My biggest concern is how the money changes values, lifestyles, and work habits after a little success, because it gives athletes a false sense of worth. They tend to forget what brought them that success. The Steelers have never been known for overpaying their players. In a strange, odd-ball way, that wound up motivating the Steelers in the glory years because our players were hungry. Some had incentive clauses that kicked in if we made the playoffs. And we could smell that playoff cash. We always knew if we got to the Super Bowl, that meant another thirty grand. It kept our attention.

There is another side to the Big Bucks Syndrome. I don't know if I could have played for two million dollars because the pressure of staying healthy and extending my career might have been too great. I don't know how it would have affected my life on or off the field.

Somebody needs to wake up the NFL owners before their game goes bankrupt. I know they tried to hold the line in the 1987 players' strike, but they have a propensity for shooting themselves in the foot. By the time it reaches the negotiations stage, it's too late. If the owners hadn't been trying to give away the store, they never would have gotten into the predicament that brought about the strike in the first place.

Paying anybody two million dollars to play a game is ludicrous. Where does it end? The stadiums are not getting any larger. The TV ratings are starting to sag a bit. So how can prices keep going up? I definitely think interest in the game has topped out. Oversaturation. Football is no longer unique.

My interest in Monday Night Football is no longer there. The thought of sitting down for three hours and watching an entire game in prime time is not very appealing. I can't remember the last time I watched an entire Monday night game. My interest has waned because there's too much football available. I have a satellite dish at my home in Roanoke, Texas, and there's so much football coming at me that I'm overwhelmed. But even without the dish, you've got Monday night games, Thursday night games, Sunday night games, doubleheaders, tripleheaders, and I'm not even talking about the colleges.

Although the salaries are escalating for the Elways and the Dan Marinos, the money paid out to first-round draft choices isn't as lavish. I don't know how the Wilbur Marshall free agency situation will affect the NFL, but I doubt seriously that total free agency is even remotely close to becoming reality, despite the league's modified version introduced in 1989. It was only a charade to appease the courts. But if this is the start of free agency, they might as well close the doors to the NFL right now, because it's only a matter of a few seasons before they'll be out of business.

If in any way I have made this appear to be totally the athletes' fault, I didn't mean it. The athletes must be smart enough to recognize that when their careers are over, fans will move on to the next group of stars. But even when the cheering stops, there is the springboard effect. If you've had success as an athlete, you have a better chance to move out into society because fans love their heroes. It doesn't mean it will be handed to the ex-athletes, it only means they will have more opportunities.

If I were in a business and had a chance to hire one of two people—one an ex-jock and one not—I would probably pick the athlete if everything else was equal. I see nothing wrong with athletes becoming heroes, as long as both the athletes and the fans keep it in perspective. It bothers me, however, when an ex-football player is hired over a person more qualified because he is a celebrity.

Heroes fell hard in the '80s, from the pulpit to politics, and a good white hat is hard to find these days. There are still the Magic Johnsons and Larry Birds and Sugar Ray Leonards and the Jack Nicklauses, but the list is getting shorter.

I wonder if it's because the salaries have escalated so high that the average fan can no longer identify with the ball player. As careers are extended and salaries are raised, it becomes increasingly difficult for the athlete to separate himself, or herself, from the game. The players I feel sorry for are the ones who don't recognize from the beginning that they are just passing through and that all this is going to end one day fairly soon.

I never was caught up in this stuff about being a Steeler. I knew I couldn't play forever and that my life as an NFL player would come to an abrupt halt one day. For that reason, I was always worrying about what I was going to do when I got out. You work hard to establish yourself as a player in the hope that you will impress some big company and that it will take you on as a spokesman. But that rarely happens and there is the danger of lapsing into that handout mentality. Most of the guys who make it big after football are the kind who might have been successful anyway.

11
CELEBRITY FOR SALE: TV, AUTOGRAPHS, AND A BIG MOUTH

You don't get a college degree in Celebrity. There is no piece of paper that says "Terry Bradshaw is a football star and a certified celebrity, qualified to slap backs, sign autographs, mingle with people he has never seen before, and write his name on everything from scraps of paper to ladies' underwear." The term "celebrity" isn't easily defined, but I guess if it means that people pay you money to hang out with them, play golf, and give speeches, then I qualify.

It's not possible to make a career out of being a celebrity, however, and if you're realistic, you know your allotment of fame is going to run out before long. When I am fifty years old, for instance, I can't very well send my résumé to companies under the heading of "Celebrity for Hire." I am very grateful that people recognize me, that they remember I played pro football and feel that I am important enough to ask for my autograph. I am flattered that companies pay me rather handsomely to promote their products and speak at their sales meetings. So don't get the idea I am ungrateful for this windfall. Basically, we're talking Fame for Sale here, and quite frankly, I can use the work. But I also must be realistic about its limitations over the long haul, as must other athletes. After all, Celebrity status does not come with a lifetime warranty.

A football analyst has his good days, but the downside is that you get whipsawed by big-business politics. So much of your success in TV depends upon your direct superior, just as so much of your success in football depends on your coach. At CBS, I started out under Terry O'Neil, a capable producer and special friend. I owe him a great deal for his support and for his candid criticism in my early years. But Terry fell prey to network politics, and when he left CBS I had to start over again. The result has been that I've had to learn a different system under a different head coach—Ted Shaker. So far I've worked with three different play-by-play men—Verne Lundquist, Tim Ryan, and Dick Stockton—and each time it's like learning a new offense with new wide receivers and running backs. I'm learning, but there are certain liabilities.

In 1988, CBS paired me with Lundquist again and I was thrilled. Not only is Verne a close friend who lives in Dallas, but he's a master at using his skills without ever losing the rhythm of his play-by-play. *USA Today* TV critic Rudy Martzke called him "the best-kept secret" among network play-by-play men, but he's no secret to me. He's the ultimate professional broadcaster, and it is said by those who have seen Verne work a variety of sports at CBS: "If it moves, call Verne to do the play-by-play."

My big mouth got me to CBS. As a player I was always doing interviews with the writers and sportscasters, always available, always talking. I was cordial, sometimes funny, definitely different, and willing to say what I felt. The networks like guys who are creative, controversial, and know how to communicate. One day when I was still playing, I got a call asking me to do "The NFL Today" during the playoffs with Brent Musburger, Phyllis George, and Jimmy "the Greek" Snyder. We'd sit there on the sideline and shoot the breeze. I'd make some outrageous statements, and some of them would come true, some wouldn't. I wore my cowboy hat, sang "On The Road Again," and yukked it up with Brent. They must have liked it, because later they cornered me down in Atlanta and asked me to come to work for CBS when I retired.

I loved working with Musburger on days I did "NFL Today." Brent is definitely the star—I knew that and we got along fine because I was no threat to him. I also admire his talent. He's got tremendous recall under pressure. People think he reads all those things from cue cards, but he's a great ad-libber. It's amazing how he can keep two or three people involved in a conversation while listening to the producers in one ear and concentrating on what he's saying at the same time.

There is tremendous competition among the broadcast/ production teams within the network. You don't have a good year, they don't give you a playoff game. That might be because the color analyst and the play-by-play man didn't mesh, the production crew didn't get the right pictures, or somebody back in New York liked the way the other guys parted their hair. You never know why. Television is mystifying to me, and the intricacies of the networks, the manipulation of talent, and the high-powered politics often leave me cold. You don't go to school and learn to be a color analyst. There are no books to read. It's mostly trial and error. Putting me in a booth behind a mike without any training was like taking a horse to the track: it naturally wants to run. And so I did—far too much at first.

Former coaches and quarterbacks tend to make the best analysts because they study both sides of the football game and know all the positions. Very few linemen see the big picture. A lineman can't analyze a blitz, explain angles of attack, read defensive keys, or explain how the feet, eyes, and hands come into play or what the pass routes are supposed to accomplish. Quarterbacks are as well schooled as head coaches.

In my first years with CBS I was covering mostly southern teams, none of them any good: Tampa Bay, Atlanta, New Orleans, Houston. I found out later that we were doing these games because both Verne and I live in the South. I guess they figured we couldn't be understood north of the Mason-Dixon line and this way at least half the audience would know what we were talking about.

To say the least, I had a tendency to blab. One day I was doing a Cardinals-Saints game. It was going down to the wire in the fourth quarter, with the Saints driving to win it. It was hot and heavy. All of a sudden the guard walked in and handed Verne a note. Verne slid it over to me. It said: "Shut the bleep up! You're driving me crazy!" It was a telegram from some guy in St. Louis watching the telecast. I didn't say another word the rest of the game. That probably upset me as much as anything in my TV career. I wasn't trying to hurt anybody, I was trying to make everybody happy. But it taught me a lesson: talking too much can annoy people.

An athlete has to adjust his thinking whenever he leaves the game and joins the media. At first I tried to be one of the boys, to retain my identity as a player. But I quickly found out that can't last, especially if you are going to criticize Bum Phillips's two-minute offense or say the Saints played a lousy game. The Denver fans got upset with me for saying Elway should have gone to Baltimore when he was drafted by the Colts. But the rest of the fans around the country knew what I was saying. I guess I was questioning Elway's audacity to challenge the NFL system because I had to live under it. I was old enough to remember all those original NFL teams like the Bears and the Browns and Colts and Giants, and I felt some of the younger players didn't appreciate what they had done for the rest of us. To challenge the system like that was like speaking out against the U.S. Constitution as far as I was concerned. So I resented Elway's refusing to go to Baltimore and winding up in Denver after a trade.

I hadn't wanted to go to Pittsburgh, either, but I did. I took going to a lousy team like the Steelers as a challenge and tried to make a lousy team a champion. Thinking about it now, however, I wish I'd had the balls to do what Elway did.

So a football analyst must take his shots and live with the negative feedback. It helps if you get support from your producer and your partner. I never have to worry about that with Verne. He is the kind of guy who gives his analyst enough rope and says, "Here, go hang yourself." And I damned near did.

The next year when I was doing color for Tim Ryan, I tried to talk less—just pop in and out. I didn't like it at first. I got to thinking, "Maybe the idea is they don't want me to talk as much." I would lay out for long stretches. But as the year progressed, Tim and I were able to work out a better flow.

It took me nearly four years to break my ties as a player and realize that my obligation was no longer to the NFL but to the CBS viewer. At first I was a terrible interviewer because I was scared to death of hurting somebody's feelings. My toughest assignment was having to go into the Cowboys' locker room and interview Tom Landry after he had lost a tough game to the Forty-Niners, 31–16, in the last regular season game of 1985. Roger Staubach was working with us that day, but he didn't want to do it. I stood there with Coach Landry, looking like I was about to cry, and I almost wanted to say, "I'm so sorry you lost, Coach. Will you please forgive me for having to talk to you?"

The medium is so powerful it overwhelms me sometimes. It's not that I'm impressed with the fame it can offer you. I'm more awed by my responsibility as a broadcaster. What I might consider a harmless comment could have a damaging effect on somebody. Let's say I was covering the Tampa Bay Bucs and made a remark that Vinnie Testaverde couldn't read defenses. People would pick up on that and the next thing you know the young quarterback's intelligence would be questioned. Now I have unfairly labeled a guy and he's going to have a terrible time living that down. I have done the very thing they did to me. I don't want that to ever happen.

The other side of that issue is the pressure that teams try to exert on the announcers. I experienced that in Pittsburgh when I was doing commentary for KDKA-TV. I was no longer on the Steelers' payroll and was being paid for my opinions, so that's what I gave them. And those opinions, naturally, weren't always going to be favorable toward the Steelers, especially when they were losing more than they were winning. My critical comments on KDKA drew quick response. Joe Gordon of the Steelers publicity department began to call me and say, "Who do you think you are! You used to be a Steeler and you owe us!" All of a sudden I wasn't their Golden Boy. I wasn't their homer.

I was doing my job and I blistered them in my commentary, because it was true: Chuck Noll had a lousy team. But I wasn't supposed to say that because I "owed" them. Owed them what? Gordon even went over to KDKA and got a tape of my program when I ripped the Steelers. Then he called me again and tried to intimidate me into saying nice things about the Steelers. Finally, I just ignored him and quit caring what the Steelers thought about my work on TV. They didn't sign my paycheck anymore. My critical commentaries only served to widen the rift between me and the Steelers.

So my main jobs today are as a football analyst and a celebrity. I'm proud of my so-called fame, but I'm not seduced by it. I hope when I'm fifty I'll still be as proud of having been a professional athlete. If I were a lawyer or an engineer, I'd just be reaching my peak earning years at age fifty. As an ex-athlete, I'm washed up—unless I can develop a new career. As great as Bart Starr and Johnny Unitas were, they can't make a living signing autographs and doing speeches. The kids don't know who they are anymore. And as each year goes by, fewer and fewer of those same kids will know who Terry Bradshaw was or what he did. Their parents might, but the kids won't.

Professional golfers can always play golf. They can compete until they are seventy years old. They still have their names on the sports pages when they are senior citizens. My name is not in the sports pages anymore, unless it's in the TV columns, and I am not setting any records. My career as a football player is over. What I am doing now is making money off my past accomplishments. It is a frightening thought if I allow myself to think that it could all dry up one day.

When your celebrity star fades, so do the trappings. I can't play football anymore. I am not going to make a living as a singer. I'm not going to be making any more films with Burt Reynolds—at least none that will pay me enough to act full-time. And one of these days, CBS is going to sign another hotshot former quarterback to take my place.

The autograph business has no pension plan. There are people out there without jobs, or people with jobs struggling daily just to feed their families, so I'm not trying to drum up sympathy. I was blessed by the good Lord with talent to play football and that's the only reason I'm able to command big dollars as a celebrity. That doesn't say much good about the value system in this country, however.

So I get parts in a couple of movies because I'm an athlete. What does that say for the poor slobs who studied acting and are busting their tails waiting on tables every night, just hoping for a part to come their way? Is that fair? Is it fair for O. J. Simpson to go from football to Hertz at an enormous salary, or for Dan Dierdorf to retire from football and make big bucks announcing Monday night games? Where does it say that jocks are guaranteed a living because they can run fast, throw, kick, block, or tackle? Where does it say I can work for CBS? I had no clue I'd be on TV. My plans were to save my money, move back to my ranch in Grand Cane, Louisiana, and sell quarterhorses, because that's really all I ever knew how to do. The only regret I have about the tunnel vision—wanting only to play pro football—is that I lack the skills to do anything else. No matter how I slice it, I'm in the public-relations business.

So even though I don't play it anymore, football is still a business for me. That's why when I'm at home—and I'm on the road about half the year—I like to get away from it. If you walked into my house in Roanoke, Texas, you might be surprised at the absence of football memorabilia. No pictures are on the walls in my living room except those of my family and some prints of Indian life. No trophies—I gave them all away. I kept one of my four Super Bowl rings and gave the other three to members of my family. On occasion, I wear that remaining ring from Super Bowl XIV—usually when I'm going somewhere to sign autographs. That's about my only concession to the past, and it's a commercial one.

The point is that I never want my home to be a shrine honoring my past deeds. My home is shared with my wife and daughter, and I would rather have pictures of them on the walls than pictures of me in a football uniform. Not that I'm ashamed of anything I've accomplished in football, but I just don't want to live in the past. I was the world's biggest jock—in college my entire life was focused on becoming a pro quarterback. Now that I've done it, it's not something I want to dwell on anymore.

I deplore athletes who can never let go of their glory. It makes me uncomfortable to put myself above my friends and try to be a big shot because I played football. What am I going to say to them after we play golf? "Come on over to my house and look at my fifty game balls!"? "Wanna see my trophies?" "How about my pictures? Here I am with Burt Reynolds." Total fantasy.

I remember when a friend of mine in Louisiana got drafted by the Atlanta Falcons and became enamored with himself. He put a Falcons plate on the back of his new car, a football in the window, and Falcons decals on the windshield. I thought to myself, "This boy either has a huge ego or he is terribly insecure." Half the athletes in the NFL are consumed with the idea that, "Hey, I play for the Giants"—or Bears or Redskins or Cowboys or whatever. That becomes their persona and it opens doors for them, just like it did for me. The only difference is that I worked hard to become a good quarterback and when I finally did make it, I wasn't going to let my ego swamp me.

I'm not very proud to admit it, but I've taken advantage of being a jock. It gets you to the front of the line at movie theaters and gets you a table at fine restaurants. But I was embarrassed to admit doing it. That's not the real world and it only misleads athletes into thinking that they're immortal. They're not going to make three hundred thousand dollars a year for the rest of their lives and be worshipped by the public. The truth is that three years after they retire, they're history, brother. They'll be lucky if anybody remembers their names. The end eventually comes for everybody.

The end wasn't traumatic for me, although the way it came was painful. There were a number of good reasons why I welcomed it, including the fact that every time I passed the football I felt like a bee was stinging my elbow. I wasn't angry about my career being over after the initial shock of separation. I wasn't devastated about being out of football for the first time in nearly twenty years. I had enjoyed my career and even though I would have liked to have played another three or four seasons, I was ready to move on to something else.

So unlike many of my contemporaries who have never been able to cope outside the game of football, or who left the game stone broke, I had saved a little money, walked right into a job at CBS, and, frankly, was glad to be getting away from the jock world. The truth is, though, if I hadn't torn a muscle in my elbow, I might have hung around another four seasons. I was finally at a place where my salary was decent, although at three hundred fifty thousand it wasn't even in the top ten among veteran quarterbacks. It's a job that only requires seven months of work a year, plus off-season conditioning. But in retrospect, it would have been a mistake for me to hang on. The last thing I wanted was to be somewhere I wasn't needed or appreciated and it was beginning to look and sound like I was excess baggage to the Steelers. Plus, I had taken just about as much of Chuck Noll as I could stand.

12
THE CATTLE BARON

As soon as a guy comes into some money, he starts wondering how he can get more. Then, he's liable to decide he wants to get into the cattle market. But before pursuing such a passion, the first thing he should ask himself is: what do I know about this? In my case, the answer was nothing. Didn't even know how to read the futures on the stock exchange. Didn't know a pork belly from a pot belly. This was a case of greed: a football player seeing that calves are bringing eighty cents a pound and figuring that if he can fatten one calf up to five hundred pounds, he can make some easy cash. Won't cost him a nickel and he'll make a killing in this cattle business. So after my first few years of making decent money in pro football, I was ready to start from scratch and become a genuine bona fide Louisiana cattle rancher. Rich cattle rancher. Cattle baron. Sort of a Louisiana Lorne Greene.

First you have to buy some land. In my case, I needed one hundred sixty-five thousand dollars worth of land. Now when you buy land and you're going to work cattle, the first thing you have to do for proper management is section it off so that you can rotate the cattle from one forty-acre pasture to the next. You also must be careful that the cattle don't eat the grass all the way to the ground—if they do, they'll start getting parasites in their stomachs.

In each section of the pasture land there must be a tank. Of course you have to build the tanks, so you get a bulldozer, build your eight tanks, and dig some ponds for water. Now you've got to go out and buy some barbed wire for the cross fence, which is very expensive—about thirty-two dollars a roll—you figure you'll need a boxcar of the stuff. Next you have to buy a bunch of two-hundred-dollar aluminum gates, but they have to be at least sixteen feet wide so you can get a big bush hog and hay-baling equipment through them. Don't forget the creosote-soaked corner posts to hang the gates on. Of course, you need some hammers and at least forty staple-pullers, because you're going to constantly be leaving those staple-pullers in the grass, the grass is going to grow up around them, and you'll lose them. It goes without saying that you'll need at least forty pounds of staples, enough to last you fifty years. Always buy more than you need. It's the American way.

When you handle barbed wire, you need gloves. Not just any old work gloves—good leather gloves. Knowing that you're going to leave your good leather gloves outside and lose them, you buy at least a dozen pairs.

So now you've got a hundred and sixty-five thousand bucks in land, all these leather gloves, fifty pounds of staples, two thousand creosote-soaked corner posts or cross-ties, a hundred rolls of barbed wire, and thirty sixteen-foot aluminum gates. With the forty to fifty thousand invested in these fences you're going to build, the cost of the bulldozer, the loan from the Federal Land Bank for the acreage, and the hundred grand from the Production Credit Association (P.C.A.) to buy the cattle, you've now invested well over three hundred thousand dollars.

Ready to roll! Now you're ready to buy these cattle that are going to make you rich. But how do you buy cattle? Well, through a cattle agent, of course. See, you get this cattle agent because you don't know anything about cattle, where to buy them, or how much to pay for them, or even if they are supposed to have two sets of teeth.

First thing you learn from your agent is that you can't buy just any old cattle; you've got to buy some "long ears." Now I'm getting pretty smart; I've got me an agent and I've been in the cattle business, oh, a good three days. I find out that "long ears" or "longs" or "humps" or "humpbacks" are what you call Brahma cattle. Down south we like to say "Braymer" because it will reassure the Yankees who might eventually want to buy these cattle, that we are stupid. You tell a Yankee you're working Braymer cattle, or humps, and right off the bat when you talk like that they know you are a genuine, bona fide, kick-ass cattleman who probably doesn't have a clue about how much you should sell them for.

My agent tells me the best cattle are in south Louisiana. I tell him I prefer black Braymers, what they call "Brangus," half Braymer and half Angus. I want a uniform herd that I could be proud of—you know, like show cattle. I don't want to invite my friends out to my ranch and have them look out the back door at a bunch of spots and plaids and reds and yellows and creams and blacks and baldies and whitefaces. I want me a uniform herd. And wouldn't you know it? My cattle agent just happens to know where he can put his hands on a uniform herd of two hundred twenty-five Braymer heifers that are only eight months old.

It's a mystery where they came from or how they got them, but we ended up somewhere down in south Louisiana and there they were. Never seen such a fine bunch of cattle in my life. My agent confirms this, telling me this is certainly the finest bunch of cattle he's ever seen, that they'd make me proud to own them and I'd get rich. I could just about smell the money.

What he didn't tell me is that a Braymer doesn't usually breed until she's three years old, which means I've got a hundred grand tied up in a bunch of eight-month-old freeloaders that won't be reproducing for another twenty-eight months. I got a hundred-thousand-dollar note on them and

I've got to carry that thing more than two years before I see a nickel's return on my money.

I am learning all the time about this cattle business and one of the amazing things I discover is that Braymer heifers can run like Bo Jackson. This is especially distressing when you have gone out and bought some bulls to service these heifers, because when one of those heifers comes in heat, every bull in the place is standing in line or chasing her across the pasture. Most Braymer heifers have wide-receiver speed, somewhere in the 4.3 range for the forty-yard dash. There's not a thoroughbred racehorse alive that can outrun a Braymer heifer. And there's not a jumping horse alive that can clear a twelve-foot fence better than a Braymer heifer. You think deer can jump? Braymers give clinics to deer on how to jump fences. Mama deer will bring her baby up to the pasture and will say, "Pay attention to how that bitch clears this fence. That's how you do it, son."

Learning about heifers is part of your education. You got a college degree in P.E., but now you're gonna get a Ph.D. in cattle. You're a pro football player, but now when people ask you what you do for a living, you can say: "I'm in 'kittle.' "

"What kind of kittle you runnin'?" they ask you.

"I'm runnin' Braymers."

By "runnin' " I don't mean chasin', although I did a good bit of that, too. When you ask, "What are you runnin'?" you mean what brand of cattle do you own, or what are you operating. But you don't say "operatin' " because nobody would understand you. The Yankees would understand you, but the Southerners wouldn't. To Southerners, the operative word is "runnin'."

"I'm runnin' Braymer kittle."

Turns out these Braymers are runnin' me three hundred thousand dollars in the hole. And I still haven't bought all the necessary equipment, because there's still the hay to bale.

To fully appreciate my dilemma, maybe I should first tell you of my shorthorn experience, because I learned about them the hard way before I wised up and got Braymers. Not knowing much about cattle, I called a guy named Jack at KWKH, a radio station in Shreveport. Old Jack was a big talker and he seemed to know everything about livestock. (I have a knack for finding these well-informed friends.) He suggested I drive over to Shreveport from Grand Cane and we'd ride together to the North County Livestock Auction. "Maybe you can pick up some shorthorn cattle," Jack said. When we got there, I was stunned to learn these shorthorns sold for eighteen hundred apiece.

"Too rich for my blood, Jack," I said. But Jack was the kind of guy who loves helping out a friend. As a matter of fact, Jack just happened to have some shorthorns for sale himself back at his place—twenty-two of them—and it amazed me that I could buy them from him at less than eighteen hundred each. Jack even threw in two baby calves. I got them home, began working them, and after a while I made an interesting discovery: they only have one set of teeth. "Holy mackerel," I screamed, "she ain't got no uppers." They only have bottom teeth.

That wasn't the worst part. Winter hit, my cattle came down with pneumonia, and the babies died. So I got rid of the shorthorns to the tune of about a ten-thousand-dollar loss. I got smart, though, because then I went out and bought me two hundred and twenty-five head of Braymer cattle.

Oops, I almost forgot to tell you about my official cattleman's hat. Every cattleman's got to get him a P.C.A. hat from the Production Credit Association. They are the people who loan you the hundred thousand dollars to buy these cattle. And you treasure that hat because that sucker is going to cost you an arm and a leg before you're through. So you need to be nice to the P.C.A. people and you also can be sure the Federal Land Bank people are going to be in the area, too. In case they stop in, you get a Federal Land Bank hat.

You can see that this is a going concern because you got two new hats.

Now you need some shirts, but they have got to be Levi shirts. No self-respecting cattleman would be seen without

Levi shirts. Next comes the proper footwear. I know you're thinking I should have worn cowboy boots, but they weren't practical. Flat-heel work boots or sneakers are better when you're trying to outrun cattle. See, those Braymers have a tendency to chase after you. You've got to be quick on your feet, able to jump over barbed wire fences with a single bound. Sometimes I'd wear my Spalding football shoes with cleats so I could dig in. I needed traction in case those cattle came at me. I could really boogie in that pasture wearing those football shoes. Looked like a white Lynn Swann.

Naturally I wore jeans, but they had to be Lee jeans—they were loose so when you made your cuts when the cattle were chasing you, your leg muscles wouldn't be restricted. They allow you the freedom to run and jump, which is something you raise to an art form in the cattle business. And when those cows kicked you in the ass, those loose jeans kept it from hurting so bad.

Finally, I get me some good chewin' tobacco—always Red Man chewin' tobacco. Now you're ready to associate with fellow cattlemen.

It's time to bring these Braymer kittle home to my fifty thousand dollars worth of fences and gear on a hundred and sixty-five thousand bucks worth of dirt financed by the Federal Land Bank. I got my ponds dug for water. I got my P.C.A. hat, because they loaned me a hundred grand to buy these cattle, even though I didn't pay a cent down. (I don't know what I used for collateral. I think I got it on my name.) I got my leather gloves, Levi shirts, Lee jeans, Spalding football shoes, and sneakers. And baby, I'm ready to make myself some big-time money.

I should have known this thing wasn't going to work out from the get-go, because from the very first night as a Braymer kittleman, my luck was bad. The guy I bought the cattle from showed up at my ranch about eleven o'clock at night. I hear these air brakes up the road, look outside, and here come these cattle vans.

"Mr. Bradshaw?" the guy says. "I got these cattle here."

"Won't they keep until morning?"

"No, they can't live on these vans overnight. We'll just go ahead and let them out tonight."

I noted that the vans were about thirty feet long and wondered if the cattle would be able to get out without being injured, or if they might panic.

"Oh, these cattle are pretty tough," he assured me. "They'll come out of here with no problem."

He backed those vans up and dropped that big metal gate out of that truck, and here come those Braymers.

Stampeding.

They're leaping eighteen feet out of that truck like sailfish, landing on their necks and heads, falling out sideways, totally out of control. These cattle are trampling over the barbed-wire fences, knocking down the aluminum gates, and spreading to every corner of my hundred-and-sixty-five-thousand-dollar piece of land. I had forty acres of land back there I wanted to clear off anyway, but when the cattle stampeded, they cleared it out for me. You could have heard them fifty miles away, and that's about how far they ran— fifty miles away. They ran and ran and ran. Right through and over my new barbed wire fences and aluminum gates. And probably over some of my staple pullers I'd lost in the grass, too. I just sat there and listened to them as they faded away in the pasture, all one hundred thousand dollars of them.

I never did find some of them and I'm still hoping the rest will show up someday. Every now and then, stray cattle will still come out of the swamps of Louisiana and just stare at my land. Occasionally one of the strays will walk up to me and say, "Hi, Terry. Remember me? I'm one of the bunch that broke all those fences that night you let us out back in 1974. We're all over here in the swamps, Terry, eating acorns and having a good time. Sorry about your fence. See you later."

I'd bought two hundred and twenty-five cattle and was lucky if I had two hundred of them left. But the fun was just starting. Naturally you've got to cut hay, so I went out and spent sixty thousand dollars for a John Deere tractor and another six or seven grand for a good hay baler, because I am going to fatten up these cattle and knock down some huge dollars when I take them to market. Before you bale this hay, of course, you have to cut the grass, so you buy yourself a fancy ten-thousand-dollar cutter. You think you're all set when the salesman tells you you're short one more item: a mower conditioner.

"Well, Terry, if you bale that hay and you cut it with a regular cycle cutter, that grass has got to lay there three days because you haven't broken the stems to let the moisture out, so you're going to have to get you a mower conditioner," says the salesman. Why, of course.

Another fifteen grand. So now I got a hundred thousand dollars worth of mowing equipment to cut hay for two hundred and twenty-five cattle, twenty-five of which I can't find, which now means I'm four hundred grand in the hole. Half the herd is over there in the swamp laughing at me. And I can't even get any babies for another two years.

Now I got this cattle business by the throat—it was time for expansion again. Naturally, if you're going to breed cattle, you got to have some daddies to go along with your two hundred mamas. I always seem to be able to find advice whenever I need it. An ol' boy told me, "Terry, you got all them crossbred heifers, what you need is some good Angus bulls."

I said, "Is that right?"

He said, "Yup, put some Angus bulls on them, because they'll service all of them cows and you'll get some great babies."

So they sold me twenty Angus bulls. I am dead broke. I put those bulls out there the next year, they chase those fleet-footed heifers around the pasture, and out of two hundred cows next spring I get just forty calves.

That spring, one of those forty babies and its mama come up to the house, because they are starting to feel sorry for me. Mama says, "There he is, honey, that stupid fool that went into all that debt to buy us." And the baby says, "How do you know him, mama?" And mama says, "I can tell by that P.C.A. hat he's wearing. It looks a little worn and Terry has aged a little, but that's him all right."

By now I've figured out this cattle business wasn't all it was cracked up to be. So I called an ol' boy in Oklahoma and told him to come pick them up for half what I paid for them. I lost fifty grand and I was glad to get them out of there. And all I've got to show, after I sell my tractors and mowers and stuff, is some fences and maybe a few stray cattle that still may show up at my back door some day. And, of course, my P.C.A. hat.

13

IF YOU SEE BURT REYNOLDS, TELL HIM I SAID HELLO

Making movies has always fascinated me, but I suppose it's like everything else in life: if you do it for a living, it becomes hard work.

My acting career started because of Burt Reynolds. Reynolds portrayed me as a dumb country hick with okra for brains on a TV satire during Super Bowl X week in Miami. Evidently he did a pretty good job of acting—I never saw it— because my mother was so irate she could have pulled every last one of those hairs out of Burt's moustache. The network apparently received a lot of critical mail, especially from Pittsburgh, and so the next time Burt was on "The Tonight Show" with Johnny Carson, he apologized.

Back in 1976 I had just launched my country-western singing career, opening at the Palomino Club in Los Angeles. I was an aspiring Larry Gatlin or Randy Travis and this was about my third performance on stage, so I was extremely nervous. First day I was there, this horseshoe of gorgeous roses showed up in my dressing room. The card said: "Good Luck. Burt Reynolds." At the time, Burt was shooting the movie *Hooper*, and he invited me to come out on the set the

next day. When I got out there and met the guy, I liked him—
he really is a warm, considerate person, and he obviously felt
bad about hurting my feelings.

We were enjoying each other's conversation when Burt
turned to Hal Needham and said, "Don't we have some kind
of part in this movie for Terry?" Hal found this part of a guy
on a SWAT team from Houston, and we set up a time for me
to fly back to California and film it. I returned a few weeks
later and began my pursuit of the Oscar.

My first big part was a fight scene where I had to dive
through a fake window, and I hurt my elbow when I
landed—the same elbow that I wound up having surgery on
years later. I don't know if this had anything to do with the
problem that eventually knocked me out of football, but I'm
sure Chuck would have gone absolutely crazy if he'd have
known.

In my next scene in *Hooper*, I walked over to a table where
Sally Field and Burt were sitting and said, "Hey, buddy, I put
fifty cents in that juke box and all I can hear is your lips
flappin'." That led to a part in *Smokey and the Bandit* for
both me and Joe Greene, where I told Joe to go tackle a car.
And he did, by golly. We flew down to Miami for that one
scene; I think it lasted about forty-five seconds.

Then came my big break in *Cannonball Run*, when Mel
Tillis and I got to meet Farrah Fawcett. I didn't think Mel
was ever going to quit stuttering after that.

Lo and behold, I wound up in the movies with Burt Reynolds and it was great fun. All I was doing was playing to my
redneck image. Good ol' boy parts—chewing tobacco and
blowin' out windows. So it kind of piqued my interest in
acting. I did a couple of other shows. Had a part in "Hard-
castle & McCormick" where I was a bum begging for his life.
And I must say, not too bad a job of acting.

Finding show business attractive, I got into country music
one day on a dare. I bet recording manager Tillman Franks a
hundred dollars he couldn't get me a recording contract. He
asked me, "Can you sing?" It was a logical question, and

apparently I convinced him I could because before I knew it he was on the phone to a friend in Nashville. We played the guitar and I sang "Your Cheatin' Heart" over the phone.

By now Tillman had convinced both of us that I was the second coming of Hank Williams. He called Jerry Kennedy, another friend in the music business in Nashville, and said, "Jerry, I've got Terry Bradshaw here and he's a singin' sumbitch. We'd like to come up and do an album." Jerry said, "Come on up!" Hey, I had just won my third Super Bowl ring, so you know I must be one helluva singer.

I went to Nashville and in one three-hour session we knocked out an album called *I'm So Lonesome I Could Cry*. Most singers take months, even a year, to produce an album. I did it in three hours—and, of course, won my hundred dollar bet. But now I am hooked on becoming the next Hank Williams. And bless ol' Tillman Franks's heart, he knew it.

Tillman started coming around with these songs. He would say, "Terry, here's a great song and you ought to record it. It's called 'Blue Eyes Cryin' in the Rain.' " And after listening to it I'd say, "Tillman, that is a great song. We ought to record it. Boy, that's a smash hit." Two weeks later Willie Nelson would have it on the charts and I'd say, "Tillman, you are a genius." I, of course, didn't realize that Tillman knew what artists were recording which songs, so I was easily impressed with his ability to see into the future. So I had to have Tillman Franks as my manager.

Much to my surprise, my single "I'm So Lonesome I Could Cry" actually made the country charts in Billboard and Cashbox. That, of course, meant I had a whole new career ahead of me. So I began traveling around the country, doing concerts. I opened for the Statler Brothers, Oak Ridge Boys, Tammy Wynette, Marty Robbins, and I toured with Ronnie Milsap one summer for four shows. By then I had my own little band and I was a genuine, bona fide, real-life country singer. Went to the Wheeling, West Virginia, Jamboree. Sang for the governor. Got to where I would sing for anybody.

I loved my new career except for one problem: it was about

to put me in bankruptcy. It cost me so much to keep a band together that even after a good payday, I would be lucky to have any money left after I paid my own expenses. There was another problem: I was a rank amateur trying to put a show together and couldn't get anybody to help me with it. A lot of the big-name performers would say, "Sure, I'll help you out, Terry," but they never seemed to have time. Larry Gatlin came over to see my show, and when I asked him what he thought, he was brutally honest: "My brothers can sing better than you."

Things took a turn for the worse. Mercury released me from my recording contract. The producer didn't even have the guts to call me and tell me. He sent me a Mailgram.

I went back out to play the Palomino Club one night and I couldn't find Tillman. Couldn't find my own manager. So I fired him. Sometimes I was making fifteen thousand dollars in three days and having to pay out twenty thousand. I loved singing and wanted to get serious about it, but I just couldn't seem to find my niche.

So I quit singing—at least a hundred bucks to the good. I guess the upshot of all this is that one day I'll be able to say to my kids, "I did a movie—here, take a look at it" and "I used to sing—listen to my album." Maybe the truth is that I've always enjoyed just dabbling in things for the joy of it, without having to risk failure. That way you can get a little taste of it without getting involved and finding out that the competition is a whole lot more difficult than you realized. If I had pursued acting or singing on a full-time basis, I would have been held accountable. As it is, I guess, people might say, "Boy, you can really sing" or "Boy, you can really act," and we'll never really know for sure if they're right or wrong, will we?

I was fortunate in being able to experiment with a lot of careers before I settled down with CBS. And my wife, Charla, helped me achieve that. It takes some of us longer to find the right marriage partner. Finally, after failing at marriage, I found the woman I wanted to live with and have my children, someone who loves me and makes my life content. So I appreciate it more than most married men. This marriage is the greatest thing that ever happened to me.

Charla Hopkins Bradshaw is not only the woman I love but the mother of my children, my lover, business partner, and friend. I love her for a lot of reasons, including the fact that she is extremely smart, efficient, and meticulous. She is very attractive, a tremendous athlete, has a great body, is a terrific cook, a great homemaker, loves being a mama, and wants to make something out of her life. She's also somewhat independent, which I like, because I don't want to sit around and spend all my time trying to make her happy when I can't possibly fulfill her every need. For instance, she's about to enroll at SMU law school, which is fine with me. I'll support her every way I can. If she is happy, then chances are I am going to be happy, too. Since our marriage in early 1986, I have never been happier in my life. And now that we've got little Rachel, born in 1987 (and another child on the way in 1989), I feel like a complete person. When you get married and have that first child, all those Super Bowls, Super Bowl rings, fame, and attention pale by comparison.

Since my last marriage was not successful, I was more determined than ever to make this one work. Last time I think I fell in love with the image of a woman and what I wanted her to be. The first time I ever saw my former wife, Jo Jo Starbuck, she was in the spotlight. After Super Bowl IX in January 1975, some of the guys were going out to see the Ice Capades and insisted that I go along with them. Moon Mullins kept on insisting I go, so I finally relented. That night I saw her—she was wearing a green dress, and I was very, very impressed.

Some of the guys had met several women in the Ice Capades the night before and had made arrangements to go out dancing with them after the show. And I said, "Man, I'd like to meet the girl in the green dress." I was immediately attracted to her. I wanted to get to know this lady in the green dress who was the star of the show.

I wound up walking Jo Jo back to her place and asked her to go out with me. She said she couldn't because she had to go inside and make some phone calls. That was pretty crunching, but I went on my way and forgot about it.

The following year, the Ice Capades came back to Pittsburgh and Jo Jo invited me to be her guest at the show. I sat there in the orchestra pit and watched her skate: she was magnificent. After the show we went to a little restaurant and talked until two A.M. She gave me a bunch of pictures. I was starstruck. We hit it off. This time I thought I was definitely in love.

I am very demanding when I want something—I go right after it 110 percent. So I pursued Jo Jo Starbuck with an all-out blitz and finally got her to marry me in 1977.

Not only is she pretty and talented and a celebrity, but she's a super Christian. She read the Bible, prayed, wore a cross around her neck, and was loaded with religious tracts. I just couldn't be with her enough. She, of course, was traveling around the world doing ice shows, and I was traveling around the country doing football games. Every week either I would fly in to see her or she would fly in to see me. One Saturday night before a home game, I hired a driver in Pittsburgh to drive me to Cleveland where she was appearing. I slept in the back seat. When I got there I stayed up all night long with her and left Cleveland at 5 A.M. for Three Rivers Stadium. I mean, I was hooked. And when I wasn't with her, I was miserable. I was crazy about her. Life was fun again and it was exciting. The best adrenaline in the world is being in love.

Now I was beginning to see myself with a house full of kids. Except I forgot one thing. Jo Jo and I didn't really ever have a husband-and-wife relationship. We had a celebrity-to-celebrity relationship. She made me aware of my celebrity status, and after we were married I began to cash in on it, which was great. The only problem was that we were both thinking too much of our careers instead of each other. We were competitive. I wasn't willing to sacrifice our family for our careers and began to feel I was second to her profession.

Her skating was the most important thing in her life, and she wasn't willing to sacrifice it. She was gone all the time and I was lonely. Hell, I had gotten married to keep from getting lonely. And when she was home, she was on the phone all the time, either talking business or talking to her mother. That was a strain.

I often wonder if I was really in love with Jo Jo or if I was just in love with the girl in the green dress who dazzled me that night. I hate to think that it was the girl in the green dress, because I couldn't have hurt so bad and cried so much if it wasn't the real thing. Yet, when it comes right down to it, I might have very well been in love with the celebrity and not the person—my image of what I thought our marriage could have been like. I could see her living on a farm, raising a family. We tried that. We moved down to the ranch in Grand Cane, but she just couldn't ever adjust to that kind of life, which I can understand now.

To this day, I am totally confident that Jo Jo never really loved me. I felt like I was there to support her career, both financially and emotionally, and that she liked being married to a celebrity as much as I did. One of the reasons she got married was that she and her skating partner were splitting up, and he was going back to college.

Jo Jo began to spend less and less time at the Louisiana ranch. She was always flying off to see her mother in California or to an ice show in New York. We didn't have a marriage. We had long conversations, prayed together, tried to make it work. It never worked out.

She filed for divorce in August 1980. The police came while I was in meetings with the Steelers, called me out in the hall, and served the papers on me—it was very embarrassing. So I filed a countersuit. Then we were going to get back together, so I dropped my suit. But she never did drop hers. The end finally came months later. It was very costly, both emotionally and financially.

I doubt that many people know, or care, about my recent success in marriage, because it's good news and most people are bored by stories of happy marriages. Also, I'm no longer in the spotlight. But when I was, every last one of my failures made the sports pages, including the breakup of my marriage. I came from a family of Christians that didn't believe in divorce, so the dissolution of my marriage was traumatic. I was a failure not only in the eyes of my church but in the eyes of my family. And to make matters even worse, I would pick up the paper and read all about my failures. I retreated back to Louisiana and sat around my ranch for one whole year, thinking what a mess I had made out of my life.

So I turned anticelebrity in 1981. Went into my good ol' boy routine. Hatred was poisoning my system. I dated a bunch of different women, including my present wife. We dated off and on for four years and I treated her terribly. I didn't know if I would ever be loved again or if I could love anybody. I had a big shield up over my heart, and nobody was going to break through it. Then Charla finally said to me: "I've had enough of you and I'm going on with my life." She rejected me, and I couldn't stand it. She forced me to come to grips with my relationships. It wasn't the "love" part I had been worried about with Charla, it was the "married" part. What would it be like when we got married?

It couldn't have worked out better, except, of course, I wish I had found Charla to begin with. Now I've got a woman who wants to raise a family and loves me more than anything else in this world, a fine Christian woman who goes to church and wants to have Bible study. A woman who gives me the freedom to be myself, travel on the road with my jobs, play golf seven days a week if I want to, and asks nothing more of me except to balance the check book.

With the love and support of Charla, Rachel, and my family back in Louisiana, my life has made a complete turnaround. I would have preferred to take a short cut, of course, and avoid the pain I caused others and experienced myself, but that just wasn't to be.

I wish my Christian life could have been more private. I'm a Christian, but I run hot and cold with it, like everything else I do. I got caught in a trick bag by people who kept telling me that I should take a stand for Jesus, but sometimes I don't feel worthy as a witness. I made a speech at a church one time and a bunch of people were saved—accepted Christ. I had no business making that talk, but I did. I wrote two Christian books and recorded two religious albums, and all of a sudden I was placed on a pedestal by some people. But I didn't want to be there. I didn't ask for that.

Because I was an athlete and a visible figure, a number of my friends in the ministry often asked me to do various things. I am really uncomfortable around most of them, and I'd just as soon keep my distance—just me and my Bible and my guitar and my heart. I didn't like to be measured by others when it came to my faith, and that drove me away from a certain sector of Christians.

The chaplain for the Steelers was a guy I could never please. I didn't seem to be able to keep my promises to him, and he always seemed to let me down. I counseled with him during my divorce and instead of showing me compassion, he always seemed to take the other side. I was trying to be a good Christian at the time, but it just wasn't in me. I didn't like him at all, so I quit going to chapel.

Then there is Jerry Falwell. I was having problems and flew down to see him. He sent his jet. We traveled a bit together and I enjoyed his company. But I was emotionally spent. Then he asked me to speak on his Sunday morning program when I was going through a divorce. Here I was getting used again. So I went to church but declined to speak. I admire Falwell, though. I think he has his feet planted firmly on the foundation of what God wants him to do, although he probably wishes he had never gotten involved with trying to bail out the PTL.

Another friend in the ministry, a guy I really like, booked me into speaking engagements in Dallas, Atlanta, and St. Louis without even asking me. He dropped by my house and told me about it. I was steamed but didn't let him know it. I just didn't do it.

I have my own image of a preacher and it isn't a guy wearing a three-piece suit flying around the country in a jet and bagging money so he can build a college. My image of a preacher is a family man on fire for God. A man who lives from paycheck to paycheck. A guy who never complains, who loves people and cares about babies. A preacher who only begs for money when the offering plate is being passed around.

You can't get near the preachers today. They are all superstars. If you went to Oral Roberts University, you couldn't get near Oral Roberts. Too big. You couldn't get close to Pat Robertson. Falwell has guards around his house. They are all electronic preachers and they're big. I'm not into big. You spread the gospel by word of mouth: Christ was the son of God, he died to save us from our sins, and he will come into your heart as your personal savior if you ask him.

I don't think people can honestly accept Jesus when there is a big revival one night and it's all gone the next day. The spirit must be cultivated. A person's soul must be touched and awakened. You have to know that Christ is real. I don't think that happens often in those large gatherings where they say, "We saved ten thousand last week." Most of them just go back to their old ways. But, of course, that's the problem for all of us, isn't it?

I am constantly fighting to keep my faith strong—it's on fire one month and cold as ice the next. There is a part of me that wants to go out and set a good example for young people, but there is another side of me that just wants to say the heck with it and go play golf and drink beer with the guys.

One thing I have promised myself is that I am going to avoid making public statements that I can't back up. I sometimes cuss, and I like to have a drink with my friends without feeling guilty about it, so I'm not going to subject my family and myself to ridicule by trying to be something that I am not. I will share my faith with my friends and my family and, on occasion, with others when I am led to do it. But I am not going to allow myself to say and do things for the satisfaction of other people. And I am not going to put my faith in men—men will let you down but Christ will not. I am also not going to let people screw up my mind by telling me I am not saved, because I am saved. Sometimes I am not proud of who I am or how I act, but I *am* saved. I know because of my heart and my soul and my love for Christ and for other people.

There are a lot of confused people in professional sports, trying to be all things to all people. If I could give them any advice, I'd tell them not to commit themselves to any one special religious group or anything they don't feel they can live up to. Don't put yourself in a position of being ridiculed, although Jesus did say once you've taken a stand for Him, you're going to get knocked.

I get a little upset when somebody walks up to me in an airport and asks, "Are you saved?" I say, "Yeah, now beat it." I get uncomfortable when people say to me, "You are a fine example to the youth of America because you are a strong Christian man." The truth is that all athletes are superstitious and part of their religion serves that purpose. A football player will say, "Oh, I didn't go to chapel today," almost as if it were a good-luck charm. I was in a position to be judged by a lot of people, and it was painful. I was called "Elmer Gantry" because I couldn't live up to what some people expected of me. I hated that because the worst sin in the world is to stand in the way of another person being saved. I would rather never have been saved myself and be alive with a chance to become a Christian than to have done something in my past that kept others from finding Christ.

We have to keep practicing our faith every day, because we have such a long way to go. I know I certainly do.

14

MR. ROONEY: THE ONLY LEGEND I EVER KNEW

Maybe it was the warmth of Art Rooney that made so many people think they knew him better than anyone else did. He was special to so many of us, and he is unquestionably one of my all-time favorite people. When I was drafted by the Steelers, most of the talk when I got to Pittsburgh was about The Old Man. I didn't know who The Old Man was, except that he smoked big, long cigars, and they said he owned the team. I remember bumping into him one day my rookie season, back when he was a mere pup of sixty-nine, and one of the first things that struck me about him was the sunshine of his personality. He was always so happy and jovial, a man with a very gracious personality and many flattering comments. The full impact didn't hit me then, but soon I would grow to realize that I'd never meet another person like Mr. Rooney.

I think Mr. Rooney felt sorry for me and took me under his wing. He may have even enjoyed my innocence and naiveté —I was just thrilled to be playing in the NFL. Maybe he liked my enthusiasm, my aggressiveness. Or maybe I was just his kind of guy and he knew I genuinely liked him. I think he liked me in a way that he didn't other players. But each player was unique to him. What's special to me today about Art Rooney is the collection of his handwritten letters and the memories of our dinners together. He probably wrote me a hundred letters while I was playing, most of them encouraging me through the bad times. He would write something like this: "Dear Terry: I'm over here in Ireland and boy, they think I'm a big shot over here! You guys won the Super Bowl, but I'm the big star this year. I'm getting all these awards—boy, oh boy, oh boy, you've really got to go some now to catch up with me! I hope everything is going well with you. We'll be over here another few days, and then we're heading for New York. Call me when you get back and we'll go to the farm. Be sure and tell your mom and dad hi, and that I wish them the very best. They are such wonderful people. Sincerely, Art."

Every letter he wrote always included that line: "Be sure and tell your mom and dad hi, . . . they are such wonderful people."

We would either have dinner at his house or we'd go to an Italian restaurant that he liked. Mostly we made small talk, but he made it a point to invite me to dinner when times were bad for me. When I was depressed and down, or the press was on my back after a bad game or two, he would call and invite me out. Even after I retired, when I was publicly critical of Chuck on my TV show at KDKA, Mr. Rooney would call me and say, "You were great! You're right, they did play lousy! Tell it like it is!" And then he would laugh. I think he kind of got a kick out of my maverick style.

I always tried to get Mr. Rooney to talk about the old days of football, but he'd steer the conversation over to horses or family. Or we'd talk about problems the league was having. He would tell me things that were going to happen. He knew I'd never break his confidence. In turn, he was my sounding board. He always left me brimming with confidence. He would tell me how great I was going to be someday. He would compare me to Sammy Baugh, one of his favorite old-time quarterbacks, because Sammy could kick it and run it and throw it.

I'd often visit him at his office. We'd puff on cigars until the air was blue with smoke. Sometimes I'd go into his office when he wasn't there, take the morning paper, help myself to one of his fat cigars, and sit there behind his desk smoking it. The first time I went in there and took a cigar, I left him a dollar. He kept that dollar until the day he died; to my knowledge it's still on his desk. I don't know how many times he caught me going through his cigar box. I felt like a kid with his hand in the cookie jar, but he told me to help myself. I could walk in there without saying a word to his secretary and have the run of the place. Usually I'd read his thoroughbred magazines.

Sometimes Mr. Rooney would walk in while I was there, pull up a chair, and sit on the other side of the desk. I always jumped up to move, but he'd insist I stay there. He'd say, "You look good in that chair! That's where you ought to be sitting! You're a big shot and I'm a nobody." He, of course, was as big a shot as the game ever knew.

Mr. Rooney wasn't a real hands-on type owner; mostly his sons ran the team. But he *was* the team and he didn't have to do anything but be Art Rooney, Sr. He had people hired to take care of the rest. Besides, he was too busy being a legend. After all, he helped found the NFL. I've said this before and I'm not sure people understand it, but Mr. Rooney was a first, an original. For those of us who had the privilege of knowing him, it was pure joy. I knew only one legend in my entire life and that was Art Rooney. I can't even name you another one.

We usually dealt with Dan Rooney, who was extremely tough. But I always assumed that Art, Sr., had the final say when it got right down to it. After all, it was his football team—a team he had first purchased in 1933 for twenty-five hundred dollars. They were called the Pirates in those days and through a complicated maneuver in which he sold majority interest to a New York City cosmetics heiress, bought into the Philadelphia Eagles, and then persuaded owners of both teams to swap franchises, Mr. Rooney wound up with a minority ownership in the Steelers. Later they would be merged with the Eagles during World War II and become the Steagles, then with the Chicago Cardinals as the Pitt-Cards. But finally Mr. Rooney gained control right after the war ended. He would delight in calling himself "a Pittsburgh guy." He was a champion of the little people and would stop on the street to speak with a steelworker, a taxi driver, a doorman. They, like me, felt there was a special part of Art Rooney, Sr., that belonged to them. In victory or defeat, his personality never changed. Among Americans, that is a rarity.

Nobody ever spoke a bad word about Art Rooney and even his competitors respected him. If he beat you, he would send over a bottle of Dom Perignon—it wasn't always just the winning—he enjoyed the fight.

I began to realize that Mr. Rooney wasn't like the rest of the owners when we'd get together with other players. It wasn't until I heard them discuss their owners in real defiant terms that I realized how lucky I was to be working for a person who genuinely cared about his players. One of the Steelers would mention that hot meals were served to us in the Allegheny Club at Three Rivers every Wednesday and Thursday. And the players from the other team would say, in disbelief: "You get *what?*"

"Doesn't everybody get hot meals on Wednesday and Thursday?"

"Nah, man, we bring a sandwich."

Mr. Rooney went out of his way to make the Steelers feel they were appreciated and respected—like buying a corner lot near Three Rivers Stadium so we could practice on a dirt field and not ruin our legs on artificial turf. The more we won, the more good things he did for us.

Art Rooney was a tough character from the mining town of Coulterville, Pennsylvania, the oldest of eight children and the son of a saloon keeper. He almost drowned as a boy on his way to school. His canoe tipped over while he was trying to cross the Allegheny River during a flood. Art went down twice before finally grabbing the post of a grandstand at old Exposition Park, the original home of the Pirates. Art and his brother, Dan, were great athletes who played virtually every sport, including football, well enough to receive scholarship offers from Knute Rockne at Notre Dame. As brash young kids, Art and Dan would go to the carnivals, accept the challenge of the house fighter, and earn three bucks for every round they could last in the ring with him. Art made the United States Olympic boxing team as a 135-pounder, but decided not to compete overseas. He was a player-manager for a minor-league baseball team in Wheeling, West Virginia—Dan was also on the team—and hit .369, second best in the Middle Atlantic League. And the Rooneys got into the football business early when they started a semipro team called Hope-Harvey; among the teams they played were the Canton Bulldogs, who had a player named Jim Thorpe.

There are volumes of interesting stories about The Old Man. But perhaps the most famous story is about how he became wealthy over a long weekend at two New York race tracks. Nobody knows exactly how much he won, but in 1936 Mr. Rooney experienced one of those hot streaks every gambler dreams about. His reputed earnings were easily equivalent to more than a million of today's dollars at a now-defunct track called Empire City one day and at Saratoga the next week. He said he bet twenty bucks with a bookie in the Empire City grandstand (back when that was allowed) and wound up winning seven hundred bucks. Typically, he felt sorry for the bookie and kept betting with him to give him a chance to get even. "I had three or four winners and broke the guy," he said, almost shamefully. That following Monday, Mr. Rooney went to Saratoga with a couple of guys, including a famous sportswriter named Bill Corum, and kept his streak going. Corum even wrote a column about his incredible run of luck.

When he was inducted into the Pro Football Hall of Fame in 1964, Mr. Rooney said: "I am lucky." He would go to any extreme to avoid taking credit for anything.

Art Rooney died on August 25, 1988; he was eighty-seven years old. I couldn't bring myself to fly to Pittsburgh for his funeral. I knew it would be attended by hundreds; but our relationship was private, not meant to be shared by all those people. Someday I will go to Pittsburgh by myself. Then I will go to his graveside and shed my tears.

Mr. Rooney was the only thread that held me to the Steelers after my retirement. No one in the organization can ever take his place. He treated me like a human being—I love and respect people who treat me the way they want to be treated. There is nothing I wouldn't have done for him. Yet he never asked me to do a single thing. That's why it was so special when we won Super Bowl IX. I used to joke about winning all those Super Bowls for Mr. Rooney. In my speeches I'd say: "We won one for Mr. Rooney! God bless Mr. Rooney!" And then, "We won two for Mr. Rooney, what a wonderful man!" And when we won three: "I'm getting sick and tired of winning Super Bowls for that old buzzard." Truthfully, he was the kind of guy who could have won ten Super Bowls in a row and never change.

Isn't it funny that you don't hear players today saying they want to win the Super Bowl for their owners?

Gene Collier of the *Pittsburgh Press*, on the day after Mr. Rooney's death, wrote a touching paragraph which sort of summarized my feelings: "It was a beautiful August day of majestic clarity when the sky was mammoth, and when the breeze dusted it hard, we could smell autumn start its long approach. And here comes autumn with a big hole in it."

His death left a big hole in the lives of many people.

15

PASSING THROUGH: REFLECTIONS BY THE FISHING HOLE ON A BIG DAY IN ROANOKE, TEXAS

On Tuesday, January 24, 1989, I received the phone call I had waited for all my life. It was from the Pro Football Hall of Fame, informing me I had just been voted in, along with teammate Mel Blount, Raiders offensive lineman Art Shell, and Packers defensive back Willie Wood.

The call came in the early afternoon from Executive Director Pete Elliott, while my coauthor and I were taking a break from writing this final chapter, tossing the football around in the backyard of my new home in Roanoke, Texas.

I had declined to speak to the media about my nomination to the Hall of Fame prior to my election, and when the telephone call finally came I was overwhelmed by the honor. The conversation went like this:

BRADSHAW: Hello.

ELLIOTT: Terry Bradshaw, please.

BRADSHAW: This is Terry Bradshaw.

ELLIOTT: Terry, this is Pete Elliott . . .

BRADSHAW: Pete Elliott, how you doing, man?

ELLIOTT: Congratulations. You were elected to the Hall of Fame.

BRADSHAW: Get out of here!

ELLIOTT: Nah, you were.

BRADSHAW: You're not pulling my leg, are you?

ELLIOTT: No, I'm not pulling your leg. I'm in Hawaii right now, and we just found out the results.

BRADSHAW: Did I barely make it? (Laughs)

ELLIOTT: We don't know what the vote was, but I'm sure it was unanimous or thereabouts.

BRADSHAW: Oh, Pete, thank you.

ELLIOTT: Terry, I tell you, it is a great honor . . . first time eligible. And I know your accomplishments were great, but it's quite an honor to be thought of in that regard.

BRADSHAW: It really is, and I'm extremely excited. Thank you so much.

ELLIOTT: You may want to know who went in with you.

BRADSHAW: Absolutely.

ELLIOTT: Mel Blount went in with you.

BRADSHAW: Mel Blount? Did I pull him through? (Laughter from both men)

ELLIOTT: Willie Wood.

BRADSHAW: Willie Wood—great!

ELLIOTT: And Art Shell. You four.

BRADSHAW: Fantastic! What a great group to go in with, huh?

ELLIOTT: It certainly is.

BRADSHAW: Great day for the Bradshaws. Great day for the Steelers. I just wish Art Rooney was here with us to enjoy this. He'd get a bigger kick out of it than we will.

ELLIOTT: I know how excited you are about it, but he would be, too. He loved his ball players. This [Rooney] is the greatest of all people in sports, not just football.

BRADSHAW: I should have listened to him in 1970 when he told me I would be in the Hall of Fame someday. (Laughter) He must have known something I didn't know.

ELLIOTT: Well, he has an inside track with somebody upstairs.

BRADSHAW: I'm sure he pulled some strings.

A few minutes later after that call from Pete Elliott, I lit a cigar in Mr. Rooney's honor, with the camera of KDKA rolling in my home. The two guys from the TV station had been parked out front of my gate for several hours, waiting for an interview, even though I had asked them not to come to Dallas until I knew for sure if I had been elected. But when the call came, I was so overjoyed that I decided what the heck, let them come on in the house. So they filmed it live as I received the good news.

Thus began one of the truly magnificent weeks of my life. I never had any idea of the feelings that would well up inside me. In the first few hours after learning that I'd made the Hall that Tuesday in January, I had goosebumps the size of footballs. I felt like the hair on the back of my neck was standing up. I don't know why, but I just never realized it was going to mean as much as it did.

I've always downplayed awards, but this one would be the last I would ever receive in football.

During my first five years at Pittsburgh—there were a lot of problems, and I had a lot of growing up to do—I never thought it would be possible to attain the Hall of Fame. Frankly, I thought it was quite an accomplishment that I didn't quit during those stressful times. And I guess, the way my career ended with the Steelers, I hadn't felt good about myself for quite some time. It was very frustrating for me, as I'm sure it was for the Steelers. But I know my coach had to be proud, even though we had our differences. And I was especially proud for my family and friends. It was a great feeling, one that you very seldom experience in life.

There will be many more Steelers inducted in Canton— maybe someday they'll have to build a Steelers Annex there. Mel and I and our two teammates already enshrined in Canton—Joe Greene and Jack Ham—are really representing the Steelers coaches, players, and management of the '70s. Had Mr. Rooney been alive, I would have asked him to present me at Canton. Instead, I chose my broadcast partner, Verne Lundquist. Verne is one of the friends I treasure most in my life.

People have always said Terry Bradshaw wants to be loved by everyone—and that was true to a certain extent earlier in my life. Maybe it would be more accurate to say "liked." Is there anything wrong with that? If I find out that someone I like doesn't like me, it hurts. And yet I am very selective about my close friends.

It takes a person with a high energy level to keep up with me. I didn't have many friends when I first went to the Steelers because after practice I was still hyper and would want to go out and hit golf balls. Everybody was always tired—I could never understand that. I overdid everything. I wouldn't just go out and play a round of golf the day after a game; I'd play sun up to sun down.

Very few of the Steelers liked country music. I didn't like to party. It was my fault because I didn't really care to be buddies with my teammates, because it would have required me doing things I didn't enjoy. So I never tried to be close friends with them.

I made friends outside of football. I befriended Tom Thomas, a retired executive from Alcoa Aluminum, who loved to play golf as much as I did. Tom and his wife, Lou, were sort of my adopted relatives. We lived on the same floor of the apartment house and were friends all the way through my playing career.

Tom and Lou were my leaning posts—special people to me. They made me salads, cooked my dinner, and I gave them one of my Dachshund puppies. When I was having marital problems, they looked after me. Tom lives in San Diego now and I miss him.

I can count on one hand the number of friends I keep in contact with today and genuinely care about. One of them is Dick Compton, a former player with the Detroit Lions and Steelers, but I never met him until I moved to Dallas. Dick is a born comedian. And I adore his wife, Pat, because I can be myself around both of them. Dick strokes my ego sometimes, but he'll also put me in my place. If I'm not treating people right, he'll tell me about it. He's the first friend I've ever had who will do that.

Dick is a good, solid, loyal guy. He and former Miami Dolphins running back Norm Bulaich, who lives near Fort

Worth, are my two best buddies right now. You can't be a
buddy to much more than a couple of people at a time. Norm
and his wife, Susie, and Dick and his wife, Pat, were part of a
small group of friends that celebrated with us the night after
I was elected to the Pro Football Hall of Fame. It was such a
pleasure to have them with me at a time like that.

My friends know me as a bit of a prankster. I called
Compton at three o'clock one morning and told him that the
load of dogs he ordered had arrived and asked where I could
leave them. I called Verne Lundquist and told him I had a
load of firewood that his wife had ordered—twenty-five
tons—and asked how I could get to his house. Friends are to
pull pranks on and tell little white lies to. You fib to a friend
just to have a bit of fun, because he, or she, will forgive you.
You can let the air out of his tires, set meetings for lunch and
not show up, then laugh about it when they get mad at you,
because if you give them a little hug, all is forgiven. Those
are real friends.

I appreciate all that I have now—my wife, children, family,
home, friends—more than ever before. When I went to the
hospital in October 1988, and they started checking me out
for a tumor or heart trouble, I suddenly realized how fragile
a future can be. Never mind that I might have died if there
had been a tumor in my chest. Even to have been disabled
would be disastrous, because I am basically a public
speaker and TV sports analyst, and so if I don't talk, I don't
get paid.

There's a tendency by people like me, who have never
really had a career, to work out of fear, worrying that
people might forget you if you don't keep humming. So
when you hit on something that you like and that pays good
money, you overindulge. Instead of taking a few speeches a
month, I went the limit—ten, twelve, fifteen. I was doing the
speeches in the spring and summer, then traveling Friday,
Saturday, and Sunday for CBS in the fall. I also had a TV
show Mondays on KDKA. Since Tuesday, Wednesday, and
Thursday were open, I started booking speeches then, too.

I was on my way down to Miami to give a speech in early

October and my chest started killing me. This had happened to me once before, five months earlier. But after getting a cardiogram and checkup, I was told that the pains were apparently unrelated to my heart. So I went ahead with the speech in Miami, although I had told the people there I felt I was having a heart attack and would like to go to the hospital. They told me, "You're just hyperventilating because you're nervous about the speech." I explained to them that I wasn't nervous about the speech, because I had given hundreds of them, and that I was seriously concerned about my health. They insisted I sit down and take deep breaths, that I would be okay. If I couldn't give the whole hour speech, they said, just give half of it. I was still sweating and hyperventilating, but I got up and spoke fifty minutes. Then they rushed me to the hospital. One doctor came in and said he thought I might have had an artery to my heart close up. That, of course, nearly gave me a heart attack in itself.

The tests all came out negative, so they released me. But I was still having the chest pains. They said it might have been stress-induced and that I was near exhaustion.

When I arrived back in Dallas, I had more extensive tests. While I was playing golf with Don January, the doctors called me on the course to say I had to come into the office right away. They told me I either had a tumor on my aorta or a weakness in the aorta that was about to burst. They did a complete CAT scan and called in a heart specialist.

Now I am one scared boy. I had just built this brand new home, had all this debt, had found a career as a speaker, my life seemed to be hectic but good, and now I say to myself: "Jiminy Christmas, I'm forty years old, I'm in great shape, I work out regularly, and now I'm going to die!"

The heart specialist said it didn't appear to be a tumor. So they did more tests. On the morning of October 23, while awaiting the test results, I decided that I was going to go out and run my usual six miles, heart problem or no heart problem. Everybody thought I was crazy. At times my chest hurt, but running has always been a release of stress for me and I felt better. I figured if I was going to die, I'd at least die with my sneakers on.

Meanwhile, the doctors told me that I must have two solid weeks of rest. During this time I had Charla call the people with whom I had contractual obligations and advise them of my condition. Since I did a weekly show for KDKA, naturally we had informed them, too. I never told anybody I had a tumor, but when the word was mentioned in conversation, a young guy at KDKA picked up on it and broke the story on the weekend of October 22 and 23. Then KDKA came to my house with a camera crew and began ringing the bell at the gate. I was sedated and couldn't even talk. So they asked Charla to come down to the gate and "give us a reaction from a concerned wife." She asked them to leave.

At one point earlier that month, when the stress was overwhelming me, I broke down and cried while I was sitting on the stairs. I was about to leave for another road trip—I'd hardly been home at all. I looked at my baby girl, Rachel, sleeping in her bed, and it just floored me. Here I was making more money than I had ever made in my life, but I had no time for my family.

All during this time I kept wondering if I wouldn't be happier back on my ranch in Louisiana, maybe only making four speeches a month, and playing golf and fishing the rest of the time. I probably would be happier for myself but not for my family. It is very important to me to be a provider for my family and my zeal to do that overrides my yearning for the easy life. Plus, I like knowing that I've got a career now, and I want to capitalize on it while I'm enthused about it.

I've often justified an early death for myself by saying, "How gallant that is, that a man would work so hard that he would die trying to provide for his family." That, of course, is absurd—and I certainly don't wish to die a martyr's death. It's admirable, but it's not that admirable. But it's tough to balance it all sometimes. I seemed to get a late start in life on some things, however, and I'm trying to make up for some of my bad decisions earlier in life.

Meanwhile, I got even more angry that my superiors at KDKA never even called, but their news department released a story that was incorrect. Even if it had been true, it should only have been released by the Bradshaw family or by a doctor at a press conference. After my last show, I severed my relationship with KDKA. Although for the most part I've always gotten along with the media, it wouldn't really bother me if I didn't have to deal with reporters again.

I've got a bad habit of putting things behind me when I'm done with them. But at least two of my former teammates, Joe Greene and Mike Webster, won't let me forget about them; both called when they learned I might be seriously ill. It's my own fault that I don't hear from more of them, because I haven't gone out of my way to keep up with them. I wasn't bent out of shape that I didn't hear from others; they've got their own problems to worry about.

I didn't get to talk to Joe, but I did speak with Mike, who told me he was gravely concerned and was praying for me. Mike also told me he wished more than anything that someday Chuck Noll and I could get back together. I told him that I would be glad to do it, but we'd have to have a mutual agreement, and I didn't know if it was going to happen.

I don't talk to many former teammates. I occasionally speak with Rocky Bleier and always enjoy that. During the Hall of Fame ceremonies, Mel Blount and I had a chance to renew acquaintances. That was one of the best things about getting voted into Canton: it started me thinking about my old teammates. My care and concern for them has always been there even if I didn't show it, and if I saw all those guys I'd want to hug every one of them. There is a bond among us that can never be broken, regardless of our differences.

Finally they concluded my problem was only scar tissue, apparently from when I was hit in the chest by a ball as a young boy and broke my sternum—or possibly from a football injury. The chest pains stopped about a week later.

As I close out this book and reflect on the past, it strikes me that my personal life is truly stable for the first time since I left football. It is the happiest time in my first forty-plus years. The Lord has showered me with blessings that I don't necessarily deserve: I have a few close friends, I'm making a good income, my TV career appears to be on the upswing, demands for my speaking appearances have increased, and it was one of my absolute thrills of all time to be elected into the Hall of Fame. I can't say I'm at total peace, because I want more security for my family, but once that's done and I'm not pulling quite such a big wagon, I think my life will smooth out even more.

I'm very much motivated to stay in the TV business for another decade or longer and would like very much to receive acclaim for my work as a football analyst. And I hope to grow more entertaining and informative as a speaker. When I look across the pond in my front lawn in Roanoke—I like to call it a man-made lake—I see happy times ahead: parties, barbecues, fishing off the dock for catfish and hybrid bass with a cold drink in my hand. I see six or eight beautiful cattle out there on my twenty acres and a tractor clipping away.

I really see myself getting back into my faith before I forget where it all came from. I hope the good Lord keeps me alive long enough so that I can get solid with Him again. I've been going so fast trying to get ahead, trying to fight all these stereotypes all these years, that I sometimes get off track.

I look forward to a private time in my life—and I mean this with all my heart—when I don't ever have to hear from another reporter or photographer or member of a TV crew; when I don't have to have a security guard to keep people from breaking into my house.

I want to be a real responsible parent who can raise children to be loving and caring toward people who are less fortunate than they are. Having kids has taught me that that's the real reason we're on earth. I could go to the grave a happy man knowing that my kids turned out well.

It's also important for me to have the satisfaction of knowing that I have worked hard for whatever I have and that I have treated people the right way.

Twenty-five years from now, if I am down by this fishing

hole and some stranger walks up, introduces himself, and asks, "Who was Terry Bradshaw?" this is what I would probably say:

Terry Bradshaw grew up chasing The American Dream, knowing exactly what he wanted to do at an early age—to be a pro football player.

If you knew Terry, you'd know he was just a big kid and was hardly ever serious about anything. At an early age he saw that by being silly he could make people laugh. And he got a kick out of people enjoying his performances.

He was often misunderstood, because it took him a long time to figure out what life was all about and what he stood for. He wanted to be something special, and sometimes he thought he was special when he wasn't.

His biggest weakness was trusting people. If you told him the earth was square and he liked you, he might differ a little and say one corner of it was round, just so as not to hurt your feelings.

He loved the outdoors, didn't sleep a lot, and got up early to see the sun rise because he loved it so much. And he adored the evening, because that's when the bass were biting.

He also knew early in his life that he wasn't that good at what he wanted to do, so he knew that the only way to get better than others was to work a little harder. He was committed to excellence through hard work. When he believed in something and wanted it, he wouldn't stop until he got it.

He was very sensitive—easy to love, easy to hurt. He hated himself for being wishy-washy and for those few times when he might have appeared rude or abrupt to outsiders.

Terry Bradshaw was a guy who needed to stop and smell the flowers more, because that's what he really wanted to do. But he was always in a hurry to meet the next challenge because, after all, he knew deep down in his heart that in this short time on earth, he was really only passing through.

APPENDIX:
MY STATS

For those of you who are interested in statistics, the stats for my 14-year pro football career with the Pittsburgh Steelers can be found on the next page.

Born September 2, 1948, at Shreveport, LA • Height: 6′3″ • Weight: 210 • High School: Woodlawn, Shreveport, LA • Received bachelor of science degree in liberal arts from Louisiana Tech University in 1970 • Selected by Pittsburgh in 1st round (1st player selected) of 1970 NFL draft • Named to The Sporting News AFC All-Star Team, 1978

Year	G	PASSING							RUSHING				TOTAL		
		Att.	Cmp.	Pct.	Gain	T.P.	P.I.	Avg.	Att.	Yds.	Avg.	TD	TD	Pts.	F.
1970	13	218	83	38.1	1410	6	24	6.47	32	233	7.3	1	1	6	3
1971	14	373	203	54.4	2259	13	22	6.06	53	247	4.7	5	5	30	7
1972	14	308	147	47.7	1887	12	12	6.13	58	346	6.0	7	7	42	4
1973	10	180	89	49.4	1183	10	15	6.57	34	145	4.3	3	3	18	3
1974	8	148	67	45.3	785	7	8	5.30	34	224	6.6	2	2	12	1
1975	14	286	165	57.7	2055	18	9	7.19	35	210	6.0	3	3	18	6
1976	10	192	92	47.9	1177	10	9	6.13	31	219	7.1	3	3	18	7
1977	14	314	162	51.6	2523	17	19	8.04	31	171	5.5	3	3	18	10
1978	16	368	207	56.3	2915	28	20	7.92	32	93	2.9	1	1	6	8
1979	16	472	259	54.9	3724	26	25	7.89	21	83	4.0	0	0	0	10
1980	15	424	218	51.4	3339	24	22	7.88	36	111	3.1	2	2	12	13
1981	14	370	201	54.3	2887	22	14	7.80	38	162	4.3	2	2	12	7
1982	9	240	127	52.9	1768	17	11	7.37	8	10	1.3	0	0	0	5
1983	1	8	5	62.5	77	2	0	9.63	1	3	3.0	0	0	0	0
Totals	168	3901	2025	51.9	27989	212	210	7.17	444	2257	5.1	32	32	192	84

Quarterback Rating Points: 1970 (30.6), 1971 (59.8), 1972 (64.1), 1973 (54.7), 1974 (55.1), 1975 (88.2), 1976 (65.3), 1977 (71.2), 1978 (84.8), 1979 (77.0), 1980 (75.1), 1981 (83.7), 1982 (81.4), 1983 (133.9). Total: 70.7. AFC Championship Games 1972, 1974, 1975, 1976, 1978, and 1979 seasons. NFL Championship Games 1974, 1975, 1978, and 1979 seasons. Pro Bowl 1978 and 1979 seasons.